The Cybersecurity Mindset:
Strengthening Your Digital Defenses

By

Isabelle St-Jean

TABLE OF CONTENTS

CHAPTER I
Introduction

A. The Growing Importance of Cybersecurity

In today's digital age, the world is more connected than ever before. The internet has revolutionized how we communicate, conduct business, and access information. However, along with these advancements come serious cybersecurity threats that pose significant risks to individuals, organizations, and even nations. The growing importance of cybersecurity has become a critical concern for all aspects of modern life.

As technology continues to evolve, so do the methods and sophistication of cyber threats. Cybercriminals, hacktivists, state-sponsored actors, and other malicious entities are constantly seeking vulnerabilities to exploit for financial gain, political motives, or simply for causing havoc. From small businesses to multinational corporations, no entity is immune to these threats, and the consequences of a successful cyber attack can be devastating.

The rapid digital transformation across industries has further accelerated the need for robust cybersecurity measures. With the increasing adoption of cloud services, Internet of Things (IoT) devices, and interconnected systems, the attack surface for potential cyber threats has expanded dramatically. Protecting sensitive data, financial assets, and intellectual property has become an ongoing battle, requiring constant vigilance and a proactive cybersecurity mindset.

Moreover, the COVID-19 pandemic exposed new challenges for cybersecurity, with a surge in remote work arrangements and a greater reliance on digital infrastructure. Cybercriminals exploited the situation by launching phishing campaigns, ransomware attacks, and social engineering tactics to exploit the vulnerabilities arising from the shift to remote work.

The impact of cyber attacks goes beyond financial losses. Breaches of personal data not only compromise privacy but can also lead to identity theft and various forms of cybercrime. For businesses, a significant breach can result in reputational damage, loss of customer trust, and legal ramifications. On a larger scale, cyber attacks on critical infrastructure, such as power grids or healthcare systems, can disrupt essential services and even endanger lives.

The introduction of new technologies, such as artificial intelligence and quantum computing, brings both opportunities and challenges to cybersecurity. While these technologies can potentially enhance security measures, they also introduce new threats and vulnerabilities that need to be addressed proactively.

To address the growing importance of cybersecurity, individuals and organizations must adopt a comprehensive and proactive approach. This involves not only implementing the latest cybersecurity tools and solutions but also fostering a cybersecurity culture that promotes awareness, education, and a sense of responsibility among all stakeholders.

Throughout this book, we will delve into the core elements of cybersecurity, exploring best practices, advanced strategies, and emerging technologies. By understanding the evolving threat landscape and developing a cybersecurity mindset, readers will be better equipped to protect themselves, their businesses, and their communities from the ever-evolving cyber threats.

In conclusion, the growing importance of cybersecurity cannot be overstated. It is a continuous journey that requires a collective effort to stay one step ahead of the adversaries. Let us embark on this cybersecurity exploration together, strengthening our digital defenses and building a safer, more resilient digital world.

B. Understanding the Cyber Threat Landscape

In the rapidly evolving digital world, the cyber threat landscape has become a complex and ever-changing battleground. Understanding the nuances of this landscape is crucial for individuals, organizations, and governments seeking to protect themselves against cyber threats effectively.

Cyber threats encompass a wide range of malicious activities carried out by cybercriminals, hackers, and nation-state actors. From common cybercrimes like phishing and ransomware attacks to sophisticated Advanced Persistent Threats (APTs) and zero-day exploits, the threat landscape is diverse and multifaceted. These threats can target individuals, businesses, critical infrastructure, and even government institutions.

One of the primary challenges in comprehending the cyber threat landscape lies in its constantly evolving nature. Cyber attackers are agile and adaptive, continuously devising new techniques and exploiting emerging vulnerabilities. As technology advances and new devices and platforms emerge, so do the opportunities for malicious actors to find and exploit weaknesses. This constant cat-and-mouse game between attackers and defenders makes it crucial to stay informed about the latest threats and countermeasures.

Moreover, the motivations behind cyber attacks vary widely. While some attackers are primarily driven by financial gain, others may pursue political, ideological, or espionage objectives. Understanding the motives behind cyber threats can help anticipate potential targets and tailor defensive strategies accordingly.

The rise of nation-state-sponsored cyber attacks has added another layer of complexity to the cyber threat landscape. Governments and state-sponsored groups engage in cyber espionage, information warfare, and sabotage, leveraging their vast resources and technical capabilities. These state-sponsored threats can have severe geopolitical implications, and they demand a coordinated response from the international community.

The interconnected nature of today's digital ecosystem also plays a significant role in shaping the cyber threat landscape. The Internet of Things (IoT) has brought unparalleled convenience and efficiency to our lives, but it has also expanded the attack surface for cybercriminals. Vulnerable IoT devices can serve as entry points for attackers to compromise networks, steal data, or launch large-scale Distributed Denial of Service (DDoS) attacks.

In addition to external threats, insider threats pose a significant risk to organizations. Disgruntled employees, negligent individuals, or those inadvertently falling prey to social engineering tactics can become unwitting accomplices to cyber attacks.

As we delve into the depths of the cyber threat landscape in this book, we will explore the various types of cyber threats, their methodologies, and their potential impact. We will also examine real-world case studies to gain insight into the tactics employed by cyber attackers and the lessons we can learn from past incidents.

Ultimately, understanding the cyber threat landscape is not meant to instill fear but to empower individuals and organizations with knowledge. By recognizing the ever-changing nature of cyber threats and being aware of potential risks, we can take proactive steps to strengthen our digital defenses. Armed with this understanding, we can adopt a cybersecurity mindset and work collectively to safeguard our digital future.

C. Embracing a Proactive Mindset

In the face of an increasingly complex and dynamic cyber landscape, embracing a proactive cybersecurity mindset is paramount. A reactive approach to cybersecurity is no longer sufficient, as it often leaves individuals and organizations vulnerable to emerging threats. Instead, adopting a proactive mindset allows us to stay one step ahead of potential adversaries and fortify our digital defenses.

A proactive cybersecurity mindset involves a shift from merely responding to cyber incidents after they occur to actively anticipating and preventing them. It requires a proactive attitude towards identifying and mitigating vulnerabilities before they can be exploited. This approach acknowledges that cyber threats are not a matter of if but when, and it empowers individuals and organizations to take a proactive stance in defending their digital assets.

One of the key elements of a proactive cybersecurity mindset is continuous learning and awareness. Staying informed about the latest cyber threats, attack techniques, and security best practices is essential in understanding the evolving threat landscape. This knowledge equips us with the tools to recognize potential risks and take preemptive measures to protect ourselves and our systems.

Moreover, a proactive mindset emphasizes the importance of risk assessment and mitigation. Understanding the value of our digital assets and the potential impact of a cyber attack allows us to prioritize security measures effectively. By conducting regular risk assessments, we can identify and address vulnerabilities proactively, reducing the likelihood of successful attacks.

Collaboration and information sharing are also fundamental to a proactive cybersecurity approach. Threat intelligence sharing within the cybersecurity community and among organizations can provide valuable insights into emerging threats and attack patterns. By sharing knowledge and experiences, we can collectively enhance our cyber resilience and respond more effectively to new challenges.

Another aspect of a proactive mindset involves fostering a culture of security consciousness. Cybersecurity is not solely the responsibility of IT departments; it is a shared responsibility among all individuals within an organization. By promoting a culture that prioritizes cybersecurity awareness, training, and accountability, we can build a human firewall that bolsters our overall security posture.

Embracing a proactive cybersecurity mindset does not imply the elimination of reactive measures. Incident response plans and disaster recovery strategies remain crucial components of a comprehensive cybersecurity approach. However, a proactive mindset complements these reactive measures by reducing the frequency and impact of cyber incidents, thereby minimizing potential damage.

Throughout this book, we will explore practical strategies and best practices for adopting a proactive cybersecurity mindset. We will delve into various aspects of cyber defense, threat detection, and incident prevention. By incorporating these proactive measures into our daily practices, we can create a resilient and secure digital environment for ourselves and the organizations we serve.

In conclusion, embracing a proactive cybersecurity mindset is an essential paradigm shift in the face of an ever-evolving cyber threat landscape. By understanding the benefits of proactive measures, fostering a culture of security, and staying vigilant in our pursuit of knowledge, we can fortify our digital defenses and build a safer, more secure digital future. Let us embark on this journey together and embrace the power of a proactive cybersecurity mindset.

CHAPTER II
Building Strong Foundations

A. Assessing Your Current Security Posture

Before embarking on the journey of strengthening your cybersecurity defenses, it is essential to gain a comprehensive understanding of your current security posture. Assessing your existing security measures lays the groundwork for identifying potential weaknesses and areas for improvement.

Conducting a security posture assessment involves a systematic and in-depth evaluation of your organization's security policies, procedures, technologies, and practices. It should encompass all aspects of cybersecurity, including network security, data protection, access controls, employee training, and incident response capabilities.

The first step in the assessment process is to define the scope and objectives of the evaluation. Determine which assets, systems, and data are critical to your organization's operations and should be prioritized during the assessment. Additionally, clarify the desired outcomes of the assessment, such as identifying vulnerabilities, measuring compliance with security policies, or evaluating the effectiveness of security controls.

Next, perform a thorough review of your organization's cybersecurity policies and procedures. Are they up to date, comprehensive, and aligned with industry best practices? Analyze how these policies are communicated and enforced throughout the organization to ensure that everyone understands their roles and responsibilities in maintaining security.

Simulating potential cyber attack scenarios, such as phishing campaigns or ransomware attempts, can help gauge your organization's resilience and response capabilities. By conducting these simulated exercises, you can evaluate how well your employees identify and handle these threats and use the findings to improve your training programs.

Assessing the security of your network infrastructure is of utmost importance. Evaluate your firewalls, intrusion detection systems, and other network security tools to ensure they are configured correctly and are up to date. Review your access controls and user privileges to prevent unauthorized access to sensitive information.

Data protection is another critical aspect of your security posture. Evaluate your data encryption practices, data backup procedures, and data handling protocols to safeguard against data breaches and ensure compliance with privacy regulations.

Additionally, consider the security of your endpoints, such as laptops, mobile devices, and other connected devices. Assess the use of security software, such as antivirus and endpoint detection and response tools, to protect against malware and other threats.

A security posture assessment should also cover your incident response capabilities. Review your incident response plan and procedures to ensure they are robust and well-documented. Conducting tabletop exercises to simulate real-world cyber incidents can help test the effectiveness of your response plans.

Throughout the assessment, engage with key stakeholders, including IT personnel, executives, and employees, to gain different perspectives on the organization's security posture. Collaboration and open communication are crucial in understanding the challenges and opportunities for improvement.

Once the assessment is complete, compile the findings into a comprehensive report. This report should highlight the strengths and weaknesses of your security posture and provide actionable recommendations for enhancing your cybersecurity defenses.

In conclusion, assessing your current security posture is the first step in building strong foundations for your cybersecurity strategy. It provides valuable insights into your organization's strengths and vulnerabilities, enabling you to make informed decisions to protect against cyber threats effectively. By conducting regular assessments and staying vigilant, you can continuously improve your security posture and adapt to the ever-changing cyber threat landscape.

B. Establishing a Cybersecurity Culture

In the digital age, a strong cybersecurity culture is not just a desirable attribute; it is a necessity. Building a cybersecurity culture within an organization is fundamental to fostering a collective commitment to safeguarding sensitive data, protecting digital assets, and mitigating cyber threats effectively.

A cybersecurity culture goes beyond merely implementing technical security measures. It involves instilling a mindset among all employees that cybersecurity is everyone's responsibility. From top executives to front-line staff, each individual plays a vital role in maintaining a secure digital environment.

The first step in establishing a cybersecurity culture is to raise awareness about the importance of cybersecurity. Many cyber incidents occur due to human error, such as falling victim to phishing emails or using weak passwords. Educating employees about the latest cyber threats and common attack vectors can empower them to recognize and avoid potential risks.

Organizations should provide regular cybersecurity training tailored to different roles and responsibilities. This training should cover topics such as identifying social engineering tactics, handling sensitive information, and reporting potential security incidents. Moreover, training sessions should be engaging, interactive, and accessible to all employees.

Creating a positive cybersecurity culture involves promoting a sense of shared responsibility. Employees should feel comfortable reporting security concerns and incidents without fear of repercussions. Establishing clear channels for reporting incidents, such a dedicated email address or an anonymous hotline, can encourage employees to come forward with their concerns.

Recognizing and rewarding cybersecurity best practices can reinforce the desired behaviors within the organization. This can be achieved through employee recognition programs, acknowledging individuals or teams that demonstrate exemplary cybersecurity practices, and contributing to a safer digital environment.

In addition to training and recognition, leaders within the organization should lead by example. Executives and managers should actively participate in cybersecurity initiatives and demonstrate their commitment to security best practices. When employees see that cybersecurity is a top priority for leadership, they are more likely to take it seriously themselves.

Promoting open communication and collaboration between IT teams and other departments is essential for building a cybersecurity culture. IT teams should work closely with business units to understand their specific needs and challenges, enabling them to tailor security solutions that align with the organization's goals.

Beyond internal efforts, organizations can engage employees and the broader community in cybersecurity awareness initiatives. Hosting cybersecurity workshops, participating in community events, and sharing cybersecurity tips through social media channels can extend the organization's influence in promoting cybersecurity awareness.

Building a cybersecurity culture is an ongoing process that requires continuous reinforcement and improvement. Regularly evaluating the effectiveness of cybersecurity training and awareness programs can help identify areas for enhancement. Soliciting feedback from employees and incorporating their suggestions can also contribute to a more inclusive and effective cybersecurity culture.

In conclusion, establishing a cybersecurity culture is not a one-time project but a journey that requires dedication and commitment. By fostering awareness, promoting shared responsibility, and providing ongoing training and support, organizations can create a cybersecurity culture that strengthens the organization's overall security posture. Embracing a cybersecurity culture is not only a best practice; it is a crucial element in the fight against cyber threats and building a safer digital world.

C. Identifying Critical Assets and Vulnerabilities

In the realm of cybersecurity, knowledge is power. To build a robust defense against cyber threats, organizations must first identify their critical assets and vulnerabilities. By understanding what is most valuable and where weaknesses lie, they can prioritize their efforts and allocate resources effectively to protect against potential attacks.

The first step in this process is conducting a thorough inventory of all digital assets and systems within the organization. This includes not only hardware and software but also data, applications, and network infrastructure. Categorizing assets based on their criticality and sensitivity allows organizations to focus on protecting their most valuable information.

Critical assets can vary depending on the nature of the organization. For a financial institution, customer financial data and transaction records may be of utmost importance. For a research institution, intellectual property and sensitive research data could be the crown jewels. Identifying these critical assets helps direct security efforts to safeguard what matters most.

Once the critical assets are identified, organizations must assess the vulnerabilities that could potentially compromise them. Vulnerabilities can arise from various sources, such as outdated software, misconfigurations, lack of access controls, or human error. Vulnerability assessments and penetration testing can be valuable tools in identifying weaknesses within the organization's infrastructure.

An effective vulnerability assessment involves using automated tools to scan networks and systems for known vulnerabilities. Simultaneously, manual assessments may be conducted by cybersecurity professionals to detect more nuanced and emerging vulnerabilities. The combination of automated and manual assessments provides a comprehensive view of the organization's security posture.

Threat modeling is another essential technique to identify potential vulnerabilities proactively. By analyzing potential attack scenarios and mapping out potential attack vectors, organizations can anticipate how adversaries might exploit their systems and develop mitigation strategies accordingly.

As cyber threats continually evolve, organizations must regularly reassess their critical assets and vulnerabilities. New technologies, software updates, and changes in the threat landscape can introduce new risks and attack vectors. Continuous monitoring and periodic assessments are crucial to staying ahead of potential threats.

In addition to internal assessments, organizations must also consider the security of third-party vendors and partners who may have access to critical data or systems. Evaluating the security posture of third-party vendors is vital to ensure that they meet the same stringent security standards as the organization itself.

Once critical assets and vulnerabilities are identified, organizations can develop a risk management strategy that includes prioritizing security measures, implementing controls, and allocating resources effectively. A risk-based approach allows organizations to focus on the most significant threats and vulnerabilities while optimizing resource allocation.

In conclusion, identifying critical assets and vulnerabilities is a foundational step in building strong cybersecurity defenses. By understanding what needs protection and where weaknesses lie, organizations can develop a targeted and effective security strategy. Regular assessments, threat modeling, and a risk-based approach are essential components of a comprehensive cybersecurity program that adapts to the evolving threat landscape. Through diligent efforts to protect critical assets and address vulnerabilities, organizations can create a more resilient and secure digital environment.

CHAPTER III
Understanding the Adversary

A. Profiling Cyber Threat Actors

In the vast and complex world of cybersecurity, understanding the motives, tactics, and profiles of cyber threat actors is crucial for developing effective defense strategies. Cyber threat actors encompass a wide range of individuals and groups with diverse intentions, capabilities, and resources. Profiling these threat actors enables organizations to anticipate and respond to potential attacks more effectively.

❖ Script Kiddies: Script kiddies are typically inexperienced and low-skilled individuals who use pre-existing hacking tools and scripts to launch simple attacks. They are driven more by curiosity or the desire to gain recognition among their peers than by financial or malicious motives. While their attacks may not be highly sophisticated, they can still cause disruptions and compromise poorly protected systems.

❖ Hacktivists: Hacktivists are motivated by political or ideological beliefs and use cyber attacks as a form of digital activism. They target organizations and institutions they perceive as oppressive or against their cause. Hacktivist attacks often involve website defacements, data breaches, or Distributed Denial of Service (DDoS) attacks to make a statement or raise awareness.

❖ Cybercriminals: Cybercriminals are motivated by financial gain. They use various tactics, such as phishing, ransomware, and credit card fraud, to exploit individuals and organizations for monetary purposes. Cybercriminals often operate in sophisticated criminal networks and continuously adapt their tactics to evade detection.

❖ State-Sponsored Actors: State-sponsored actors are typically government-backed groups with substantial resources and technical capabilities. They conduct cyber espionage, information warfare, and sabotage to further their nation's political, economic, or military interests. State-sponsored attacks can be highly sophisticated and well-coordinated.

❖ Advanced Persistent Threats (APTs): APTs are long-term, targeted cyber attacks that aim to breach an organization's network and maintain access undetected for extended periods. APTs are often carried out by nation-state or well-funded groups. Their objectives range from stealing sensitive data to undermining national security.

❖ Insider Threats: Insider threats arise from individuals within an organization who misuse their access and privileges for malicious purposes. Insider threats may be employees seeking financial gain, individuals coerced into sharing sensitive information, or disgruntled employees seeking to harm the organization.

Understanding these different threat actor profiles helps organizations tailor their cybersecurity measures and defenses accordingly. For example, implementing strong access controls and monitoring for unusual behavior can help mitigate insider threats. Employing advanced threat detection tools and network segmentation can help defend against APTs.

Furthermore, threat intelligence plays a crucial role in understanding threat actors' activities and intentions. Continuous monitoring of threat intelligence sources can provide early warning signs of potential attacks, enabling organizations to proactively bolster their defenses.

In conclusion, profiling cyber threat actors is a critical component of cybersecurity preparedness. It provides valuable insights into the motives, tactics, and techniques employed by different adversaries, allowing organizations to build more targeted and effective defense strategies. By staying vigilant, investing in threat intelligence, and continuously adapting to emerging threats, organizations can better safeguard their digital assets and maintain a strong cybersecurity posture.

B. Recognizing Motives and Tactics

In the dynamic and ever-evolving world of cybersecurity, recognizing the motives and tactics employed by cyber adversaries is vital for effectively defending against cyber threats. Cybercriminals and threat actors have diverse motivations and utilize a wide array of tactics to achieve their objectives. Understanding these motives and tactics allows organizations to anticipate potential attacks and implement appropriate countermeasures.

❖ Financial Gain: One of the primary motives driving cybercriminals is financial gain. They target individuals and organizations to steal sensitive financial information, credit card data, or conduct ransomware attacks. Ransomware attacks involve encrypting critical data and demanding a ransom for its release. Recognizing these motives helps organizations prioritize data protection and implement robust encryption and backup strategies.

❖ Espionage and Information Theft: State-sponsored actors and cyber espionage groups aim to steal sensitive information, intellectual property, or government secrets. They may infiltrate networks to gather intelligence, compromise communication channels, or conduct covert surveillance.

Recognizing the motives of espionage can help organizations identify potential targets and bolster their data protection measures.

❖ Ideology and Hacktivism: Hacktivists are motivated by political, ideological, or social causes. They aim to raise awareness, protest against perceived injustices, or advocate for specific issues. Their tactics may include website defacements, Distributed Denial of Service (DDoS) attacks, or leaking sensitive information. Recognizing hacktivist motives allows organizations to monitor online discussions and social media platforms for potential threats.

❖ Sabotage and Disruption: Some threat actors seek to disrupt critical infrastructure, services, or public institutions to cause chaos and undermine trust. Their tactics may involve targeting power grids, transportation systems, or healthcare services. Recognizing these motives is crucial for enhancing the security of essential infrastructure and ensuring business continuity.

❖ Cyberwarfare: Nation-state actors may engage in cyberwarfare to gain strategic advantages over adversaries. Cyberwarfare involves launching large-scale and sophisticated attacks on other nations' infrastructure, military systems, or critical assets. Recognizing the motives of cyberwarfare enables nations to strengthen their cybersecurity capabilities and develop robust incident response plans.

❖ Social Engineering: Social engineering tactics involve manipulating individuals into divulging sensitive information or performing actions that compromise security. Techniques like phishing emails, pretexting, and baiting are commonly used. Recognizing social engineering tactics helps organizations implement security awareness training to educate employees about potential threats.

To recognize and respond effectively to the motives and tactics of cyber adversaries, organizations must invest in threat intelligence and continuous monitoring. Threat intelligence sources provide valuable information about emerging threats, attack patterns, and the motivations behind various cyber incidents.

Additionally, organizations should establish incident response teams and develop comprehensive response plans. These plans should include playbooks that outline appropriate actions for different types of cyber attacks, ensuring a swift and coordinated response to potential threats.

Collaboration with industry peers and sharing threat intelligence is another effective way to recognize new and evolving cyber threats. Information sharing allows organizations to benefit from collective knowledge and identify potential threats that may have been encountered by others in the industry.

In conclusion, recognizing the motives and tactics of cyber adversaries is a critical aspect of cybersecurity preparedness. By understanding the diverse objectives that drive threat actors and the tactics they employ, organizations can better prepare and defend against potential attacks. Through continuous monitoring, threat intelligence, and proactive incident response measures, organizations can strengthen their cybersecurity posture and protect their digital assets effectively.

C. The Evolution of Cyber Attacks

The evolution of cyber attacks over the years has been nothing short of transformative. As technology advanced and the digital landscape expanded, cyber adversaries have continually adapted their tactics, techniques, and procedures to exploit new vulnerabilities and evade detection. Understanding the evolution of cyber attacks is crucial for staying ahead of the threats and developing effective defense strategies.

In the early days of computing, cyber attacks were relatively simple and often driven by curiosity or personal fame. "Script kiddies" would use pre-made hacking tools to launch rudimentary attacks on vulnerable systems. These attacks were more of a nuisance than a serious threat, but they laid the groundwork for the future of cyber warfare.

As technology became more widespread, cyber attacks started to take on a more malicious and profit-driven nature. Cybercriminals emerged, targeting individuals and organizations to steal sensitive information and financial data. Phishing emails became a popular tactic, tricking users into divulging their login credentials or financial information. Ransomware attacks also gained prominence, encrypting valuable data and demanding ransom payments for its release.

The rise of the internet and interconnected devices gave birth to a new era of cyber attacks. Distributed Denial of Service (DDoS) attacks became a major concern, as cybercriminals harnessed the power of botnets to overwhelm websites and online services. The Internet of Things (IoT) introduced a host of new vulnerabilities, as poorly secured smart devices provided entry points for attackers to compromise networks.

With the growing dependence on digital infrastructure, state-sponsored actors began using cyber attacks as a powerful tool for espionage and sabotage. Nation-states engaged in cyber warfare, targeting critical infrastructure, government institutions, and military systems. These advanced persistent threats (APTs) operated stealthily, staying undetected for extended periods while extracting valuable intelligence.

As machine learning and artificial intelligence advanced, cyber attackers started incorporating these technologies into their arsenals. AI-driven attacks could analyze vast amounts of data to identify vulnerabilities, automate phishing campaigns, and even mimic human behavior to evade detection.

The rise of cryptocurrency also played a role in the evolution of cyber attacks. Cryptocurrencies provided a means for cybercriminals to receive payments anonymously, facilitating ransomware attacks and other illicit activities.

The advent of the cloud and remote work brought new security challenges. Cloud-based services offered convenience and scalability, but they also introduced new attack vectors and potential data exposure.

Looking ahead, cyber attacks will likely continue to evolve in response to technological advancements and changing social dynamics. Artificial intelligence will become a double-edged sword, used by both attackers and defenders in a never-ending arms race. As technologies like 5G and quantum computing emerge, new possibilities and threats will arise.

In response to this evolving threat landscape, organizations must adopt a proactive cybersecurity approach. Implementing strong security measures, regularly updating systems, and investing in threat intelligence are crucial for staying ahead of cyber adversaries. Collaborating with the cybersecurity community and sharing threat information will also be essential in countering emerging threats collectively.

In conclusion, the evolution of cyber attacks highlights the relentless creativity and adaptability of cyber adversaries. Understanding this evolution is essential for developing robust defense strategies and staying one step ahead of the ever-changing cyber threat landscape.

CHAPTER IV
The Core Elements of Cybersecurity

A. Network Security

In the digital age, network security is a critical component of any robust cybersecurity strategy. As organizations rely increasingly on interconnected systems and the internet for their day-to-day operations, securing the network infrastructure becomes paramount to safeguarding sensitive data and protecting against cyber threats.

Securing Your Network Infrastructure

Securing the network infrastructure involves implementing a series of measures to protect the underlying foundation of an organization's communication and data exchange. This includes securing routers, switches, and other network devices. One of the first steps is to change default passwords and disable unused services on network devices. Weak default credentials are often exploited by attackers as an easy entry point.

Regularly updating network device firmware and software is essential for patching known vulnerabilities and improving security. Vulnerabilities in network devices can serve as gateways for attackers to gain unauthorized access and control over the network.

Segmentation is another vital aspect of securing the network infrastructure. Dividing the network into smaller segments with strict access controls helps contain potential breaches and limits an attacker's lateral movement within the network.

Best Practices for Firewalls and Intrusion Detection Systems

Firewalls act as a barrier between an organization's internal network and the outside world, filtering and monitoring incoming and outgoing traffic. Implementing a robust firewall policy is crucial to allow only legitimate traffic while blocking malicious attempts.

Next-generation firewalls (NGFWs) go beyond traditional firewalls by incorporating advanced features like intrusion prevention, application-aware filtering, and deep-packet inspection. NGFWs provide enhanced protection against modern cyber threats and offer greater visibility into network traffic.

Intrusion Detection Systems (IDS) and Intrusion Prevention Systems (IPS) are essential network security tools that detect and respond to suspicious or malicious activities. IDS passively monitor network traffic, whereas IPS can actively block or prevent malicious traffic from entering the network. Deploying IDS and IPS strategically throughout the network helps identify potential threats and respond to them in real-time.

Wireless Network Security

With the widespread adoption of Wi-Fi and wireless technologies, securing wireless networks has become a top priority. Enabling Wi-Fi encryption, such as WPA2 or WPA3, ensures that data transmitted over wireless networks is protected from eavesdropping and unauthorized access.

SSID (Service Set Identifier) hiding and MAC (Media Access Control) address filtering can add an extra layer of security to wireless networks. By hiding the network's SSID, organizations can make it more challenging for potential attackers to detect and target the network. MAC address filtering allows organizations to control which devices can connect to the wireless network based on their unique hardware addresses.

Regularly updating wireless access points and routers with the latest firmware is essential to fix known vulnerabilities and maintain the security of the wireless network.

Educating employees and users about the risks of connecting to unsecured or public Wi-Fi networks helps minimize the exposure to potential threats outside the organization's controlled network.

In conclusion, network security is a foundational element of cybersecurity that requires a multi-layered approach. Securing the network infrastructure, implementing best practices for firewalls and intrusion detection systems, and addressing wireless network security are vital steps to protect an organization's assets from cyber threats. By continuously monitoring and improving network security measures, organizations can ensure the integrity, confidentiality, and availability of their network resources.

B. Data Protection

In today's data-driven world, data protection is a critical aspect of cybersecurity. Organizations store vast amounts of sensitive information, including customer data, financial records, and intellectual property. Ensuring the confidentiality, integrity, and availability of this data is essential to maintain trust and protect against cyber threats.

Encryption and Data Privacy

Encryption is a fundamental tool in data protection. It involves converting data into a secure, unreadable format using cryptographic algorithms. Only authorized parties with the encryption keys can decrypt and access the data. Implementing strong encryption ensures that even if an attacker gains unauthorized access to the data, they cannot read or use it.

End-to-end encryption is particularly important for securing data during transmission. This method ensures that data is encrypted from the sender to the recipient, preventing eavesdropping and unauthorized interception. Popular messaging apps and secure email services often employ end-to-end encryption to safeguard user communications.

Data privacy is closely linked to data protection, especially in the context of regulations such as the General Data Protection Regulation (GDPR) and the California Consumer Privacy Act (CCPA). Organizations must comply with these regulations to protect user privacy, inform individuals about data collection and usage, and obtain explicit consent when necessary.

Securing Sensitive Information

Securing sensitive information involves implementing access controls and identity management practices to limit data access to authorized personnel only. Role-based access controls (RBAC) allow organizations to grant specific permissions based on job roles and responsibilities, minimizing the risk of unauthorized data exposure.

Multi-factor authentication (MFA) is an effective way to enhance data security by requiring users to provide multiple forms of verification before accessing sensitive information. MFA can include something the user knows (password), something they have (smartphone), and something they are (fingerprint or facial recognition).

Regularly monitoring and auditing data access logs help organizations identify suspicious activities or potential security breaches. By proactively monitoring data access, organizations can quickly respond to unauthorized access attempts and potential insider threats.

Safeguarding Against Data Breaches

Despite robust security measures, data breaches can still occur. Organizations must be prepared to respond effectively to minimize the impact of a breach and protect affected individuals.

Developing an incident response plan is essential for handling data breaches. This plan outlines the steps to be taken in case of a security incident, including identification, containment, eradication, recovery, and lessons learned.

Regularly backing up data and storing it in secure offsite locations is crucial for quick data recovery in case of a breach or ransomware attack. Backups can help organizations restore their systems and operations with minimal disruption.

Conducting penetration testing and vulnerability assessments can proactively identify weaknesses in the organization's data protection measures. By simulating real-world attack scenarios, organizations can identify potential vulnerabilities and address them before cyber adversaries exploit them.

Educating employees about data security best practices and potential risks is essential in safeguarding against data breaches. Human error remains a significant factor in data breaches, so promoting a security-conscious culture is vital.

In conclusion, data protection is a core element of cybersecurity that requires a comprehensive approach. By implementing encryption and data privacy measures, securing sensitive information, and safeguarding against data breaches, organizations can better protect their assets and maintain the trust of their customers and stakeholders. With a proactive approach and a commitment to continuous improvement, data protection becomes a fundamental pillar in building a strong cybersecurity foundation.

C. Endpoint Security

In the digital era, endpoint security is a critical aspect of cybersecurity, as it focuses on protecting individual devices like computers, laptops, smartphones, and other endpoints that connect to an organization's network. Endpoints are often the entry points for cyber attacks, making their security a top priority.

Securing Devices and Endpoints

Securing devices and endpoints involves implementing a range of security measures to defend against potential threats. One of the first steps is to deploy and maintain robust antivirus and anti-malware software on all endpoints. These security solutions help detect and remove malicious software, preventing infections and data breaches.

Enforcing strong password policies is essential for securing endpoints. Requiring complex, unique passwords and implementing multi-factor authentication (MFA) adds an extra layer of security, reducing the risk of unauthorized access to devices and sensitive information.

Endpoint security solutions should also include personal firewall protection. Firewalls monitor and control incoming and outgoing network traffic, preventing unauthorized connections and blocking malicious activities.

Additionally, organizations should consider using endpoint detection and response (EDR) tools. EDR solutions continuously monitor endpoints for suspicious activities, detect potential threats, and provide real-time threat response capabilities.

Protecting Against Malware and Ransomware

Malware and ransomware pose significant threats to endpoints and can have severe consequences for organizations. Training employees in recognizing phishing attempts and social engineering tactics helps prevent malware infections that often start with unsuspecting users clicking on malicious links or downloading infected files.

Implementing application whitelisting and blacklisting is a proactive approach to mitigate malware risks. Whitelisting allows only approved applications to run on endpoints, while blacklisting blocks known malicious applications. This approach prevents unauthorized software from executing and spreading malware.

Regularly backing up data is crucial for protecting against ransomware attacks. In the event of a ransomware infection, having up-to-date backups enables organizations to restore their data without paying a ransom to cybercriminals.

Educating employees about the dangers of ransomware and the importance of reporting any suspicious activities can help detect and respond to ransomware attacks early.

Implementing Patch Management

Keeping operating systems and software up to date is a crucial aspect of endpoint security. Cybercriminals often exploit known vulnerabilities in outdated software to gain unauthorized access to endpoints.

Implementing a patch management system ensures that all devices receive timely updates and security patches. Automated patching helps minimize the window of exposure to potential threats and reduces the burden on IT teams.

Regular vulnerability scanning and penetration testing can help identify potential weaknesses in endpoint security. These assessments provide valuable insights into the organization's security posture and assist in prioritizing patch deployment based on the severity of vulnerabilities.

Endpoint security is an ongoing process that requires continuous monitoring and improvement. Regular security updates, employee training, and proactive measures such as whitelisting and EDR contribute to a robust endpoint security posture.

In conclusion, endpoint security is a critical element of cybersecurity that addresses the vulnerabilities present in individual devices and endpoints. By securing devices, protecting against malware and ransomware, and implementing effective patch management, organizations can fortify their endpoint security and minimize the risk of cyber attacks. Through a comprehensive and proactive approach, organizations can ensure the safety and integrity of their digital assets and protect against evolving cyber threats.

CHAPTER V
Developing a Cyber-Aware Workforce

A. Training and Educating Employees

In the ever-changing landscape of cybersecurity threats, the human element remains one of the most significant factors in an organization's defense. Training and educating employees about cybersecurity best practices are essential for developing a cyber-aware workforce that can identify and mitigate potential risks effectively.

Cybersecurity Awareness Training

Comprehensive cybersecurity awareness training should be a fundamental component of an organization's cybersecurity strategy. This training equips employees with the knowledge and skills to recognize common cyber threats, such as phishing emails, social engineering tactics, and suspicious websites.

Training sessions should cover topics like password hygiene, data handling best practices, secure browsing, and safe use of social media. Employees should understand the importance of reporting security incidents promptly to the IT or security team.

Phishing Simulations

Phishing remains a prevalent attack vector for cybercriminals. Conducting periodic phishing simulations can help gauge the effectiveness of cybersecurity training and identify areas that need improvement. Phishing simulations involve sending simulated phishing emails to employees and tracking their responses. This enables organizations to identify individuals who may need additional training and support.

Role-Based Training

Recognizing that different job roles have distinct cybersecurity responsibilities, organizations should provide role-based training tailored to specific functions within the organization. IT staff, executives, and customer service representatives may each face unique cybersecurity challenges in their roles. Customized training helps employees understand how cybersecurity principles apply to their specific job functions.

Continuous Education

Cybersecurity threats and attack techniques are constantly evolving. Therefore, employee education should be an ongoing process. Regularly updating cybersecurity training materials and conducting refresher courses ensures that employees stay informed about the latest threats and defense strategies.

Creating a Security-Conscious Culture

Developing a security-conscious culture is vital for embedding cybersecurity best practices into the organization's DNA. Organizations should encourage employees to take ownership of cybersecurity and recognize that cybersecurity is everyone's responsibility.

Leadership plays a crucial role in promoting a security-conscious culture. Executives and managers should lead by example, actively participating in cybersecurity initiatives and demonstrating their commitment to security practices.

Rewarding and Recognizing Secure Behavior

Recognizing and rewarding employees for practicing secure behaviors can reinforce positive cybersecurity habits. Employee recognition programs can celebrate individuals who report potential security incidents, identify phishing emails, or adhere to password policies. Positive reinforcement encourages employees to remain vigilant and proactive in their cybersecurity practices.

Communicating Security Updates

Open and transparent communication is essential for keeping employees informed about cybersecurity updates, new threats, and changes in security policies. Regularly sharing security tips, threat intelligence, and success stories of thwarted cyber attacks can raise awareness and foster a culture of cyber vigilance.

In conclusion, training and educating employees are pivotal elements in building a cyber-aware workforce. By providing comprehensive awareness training, conducting phishing simulations, offering role-based education, and fostering a security-conscious culture, organizations can empower their employees to be the first line of defense against cyber threats. Continuous education and open communication ensure that employees remain informed and engaged in safeguarding the organization's digital assets. A cyber-aware workforce is a valuable asset in today's cybersecurity landscape, contributing significantly to overall cyber resilience.

B. Building a Security-Conscious Culture

Creating a security-conscious culture is the cornerstone of developing a cyber-aware workforce. A security-conscious culture instills a mindset where cybersecurity is not viewed as an isolated responsibility of the IT department but as a collective effort involving every employee in the organization. Such a culture is essential for fostering a proactive approach to cybersecurity and reducing the risk of successful cyber attacks.

Leadership Commitment

Building a security-conscious culture begins with the commitment of organizational leadership. Executives and managers must demonstrate their dedication to cybersecurity and prioritize it as a core aspect of the organization's operations. When employees see that cybersecurity is a top-level concern, they are more likely to take it seriously as well.

Establishing Clear Policies and Procedures

Clearly defined cybersecurity policies and procedures provide a framework for employees to follow. These policies should cover password management, data handling, acceptable use of technology, and reporting security incidents. Making these policies easily accessible and regularly communicating updates helps ensure that employees are well-informed.

Training and Education

Comprehensive cybersecurity training is essential for creating a security-conscious culture. Employees should be educated about the latest cyber threats, attack vectors, and best practices for mitigating risks. Training sessions should be interactive, engaging, and tailored to different job roles and levels of technical expertise.

Encouraging Reporting of Security Incidents

Fostering a culture where employees feel comfortable reporting potential security incidents without fear of repercussions is crucial. Implementing a clear and confidential reporting mechanism enables employees to alert the IT or security team promptly when they encounter suspicious activities or potential threats.

Incentives and Recognition

Recognizing and rewarding employees for practicing good cybersecurity habits can reinforce positive behavior. Incentive programs that acknowledge individuals who report incidents, identify phishing attempts, or demonstrate exemplary security practices can motivate employees to remain vigilant.

Regular Communication and Awareness Campaigns

Consistent communication and awareness campaigns are essential for reinforcing cybersecurity principles. Regularly sharing security tips, real-world examples of cyber attacks, and success stories of thwarted threats can keep cybersecurity at the forefront of employees' minds.

Empowering Employees to Take Ownership

Encouraging employees to take ownership of cybersecurity helps build a proactive and engaged workforce. Employees should be empowered to question suspicious activities, suggest security improvements, and actively participate in cybersecurity initiatives.

Conducting Cybersecurity Drills and Simulations

Periodic cybersecurity drills and simulations allow employees to practice their response to potential cyber incidents. These exercises help employees understand how to react to different scenarios and improve incident response capabilities.

Continuous Improvement and Adaptation

A security-conscious culture should not be static; it should evolve and adapt as the cybersecurity landscape changes. Organizations should continuously assess their cybersecurity practices, solicit feedback from employees, and make necessary improvements to stay ahead of emerging threats.

In conclusion, building a security-conscious culture is pivotal in creating a cyber-aware workforce. Leadership commitment, clear policies, training, encouraging incident reporting, incentives, regular communication, empowerment, cybersecurity drills, and continuous improvement all contribute to fostering a security-conscious culture. A workforce that understands the significance of cybersecurity and actively embraces secure practices becomes a formidable line of defense against cyber threats, safeguarding the organization's digital assets and reputation.

C. Encouraging Reporting and Incident Response

In a rapidly evolving cyber threat landscape, encouraging employees to report potential security incidents and fostering a swift and effective incident response are critical components of developing a cyber-aware workforce. Prompt reporting of security issues empowers organizations to detect and address cyber threats early, minimizing potential damage and enhancing overall cyber resilience.

Creating a Non-Punitive Reporting Culture

Encouraging employees to report security incidents begins with establishing a non-punitive reporting culture. Employees should feel safe and supported when reporting potential incidents, even if the incident was caused by unintentional mistakes. Assuring employees that reporting incidents is a valuable contribution to the organization's security efforts boosts their confidence in coming forward.

Providing Easy and Confidential Reporting Channels

Organizations should provide simple and confidential reporting channels for employees to report security concerns. These channels may include dedicated email addresses, phone hotlines, or secure online reporting platforms. The easier it is for employees to report incidents, the more likely they are to do so promptly.

Training Employees in Incident Recognition

Training employees to recognize and report potential security incidents is crucial. Cybersecurity awareness programs should cover common signs of cyber attacks, phishing attempts, social engineering, and suspicious activities. Educated employees become an early line of defense, detecting and reporting incidents before they escalate.

Acknowledging and Rewarding Reporting Efforts

Recognizing and acknowledging employees who report incidents promptly reinforces the importance of reporting. Incentive programs or public acknowledgments for individuals who report incidents contribute to creating a culture where reporting is valued and celebrated.

Swift Incident Response and Resolution

A robust incident response process is essential for addressing reported incidents effectively. Organizations should have well-defined incident response plans that outline the steps to be taken in case of a security breach. The response team should act swiftly to contain and mitigate the incident, minimizing its impact on the organization.

Learning from Incidents

Every incident presents an opportunity for learning and improvement. Organizations should conduct thorough post-incident analyses to understand the root cause of the incident and identify areas for enhancing security measures. Learning from incidents helps organizations strengthen their defenses and prevent similar incidents in the future.

Providing Feedback to Reporters

Providing feedback to employees who report incidents is valuable in reinforcing their role as active participants in cybersecurity. Communicating the outcome of the incident and expressing appreciation for their vigilance encourages continued reporting and active engagement in the organization's security efforts.

Conducting Incident Response Drills

Regular incident response drills and simulations prepare employees to respond effectively to real-world incidents. These exercises allow organizations to assess the efficiency of their response procedures, identify gaps, and refine their incident response plans.

In conclusion, encouraging reporting and incident response is vital for developing a cyber-aware workforce. By creating a non-punitive reporting culture, providing easy reporting channels, training employees in incident recognition, acknowledging and rewarding reporting efforts, and fostering a swift and effective incident response, organizations can empower employees to play an active role in cybersecurity.

CHAPTER VI
Cybersecurity in the Digital Age

A. Cloud Security and Considerations

As the digital landscape evolves, cloud computing has emerged as a transformative technology, enabling organizations to scale operations, improve efficiency, and access a wide range of services. However, with the advantages of the cloud come unique cybersecurity challenges. Cloud security is a crucial aspect of modern cybersecurity, as organizations store vast amounts of sensitive data and run critical applications on cloud platforms. Understanding cloud security considerations is essential for safeguarding data and mitigating potential risks.

Data Encryption and Privacy

One of the primary concerns in cloud security is data encryption and privacy. Organizations must ensure that data stored in the cloud is encrypted both during transmission and at rest. Cloud service providers offer various encryption options to protect data from unauthorized access, but it is essential for organizations to manage encryption keys and understand how data is secured.

Compliance with data privacy regulations, such as GDPR and CCPA, is vital when using cloud services. Organizations must understand where their data is physically stored and ensure that the cloud provider adheres to relevant data protection regulations.

Identity and Access Management (IAM)

Effective identity and access management are critical in the cloud environment. IAM controls determine who can access specific cloud resources and what actions they are allowed to perform. Implementing strong authentication methods, multi-factor authentication (MFA), and role-based access controls is essential to prevent unauthorized access and data breaches.

Regularly reviewing and updating IAM policies ensures that access privileges align with current job roles and responsibilities. Additionally, promptly revoking access for employees who leave the organization is crucial to maintain a secure cloud environment.

Secure Configuration and Patch Management

Cloud services and applications must be securely configured to reduce potential vulnerabilities. Default configurations may not always align with an organization's security requirements, so proper configuration management is essential. Regularly updating and patching cloud resources with the latest security updates is crucial to address known vulnerabilities and prevent exploitation by cyber attackers.

Shared Responsibility Model

Understanding the shared responsibility model is crucial when using cloud services. Cloud providers are responsible for securing the underlying infrastructure, while customers are responsible for securing their data and applications within the cloud. Organizations must clearly understand their security responsibilities and implement the necessary measures to protect their data in the cloud.

Data Backup and Recovery

While cloud providers offer high availability and redundancy, organizations should not rely solely on cloud providers for data backup and recovery. Implementing a separate backup strategy ensures that critical data can be restored in case of accidental deletion, data corruption, or ransomware attacks.

Continuous Monitoring and Auditing

Continuous monitoring and auditing are essential for cloud security. Monitoring tools and log analysis help detect suspicious activities and potential security incidents in real-time. Regularly auditing cloud resources and configurations ensure that the cloud environment remains compliant with security policies and best practices.

Vendor Risk Management

Before selecting a cloud service provider, organizations should conduct thorough vendor risk assessments. Evaluating the provider's security practices, data protection policies, and compliance certifications helps ensure that they meet the organization's security requirements.

In conclusion, cloud security is a critical aspect of modern cybersecurity in the digital age. By focusing on data encryption and privacy, implementing strong IAM practices, ensuring secure configuration and patch management, understanding the shared responsibility model, maintaining data backup and recovery procedures, conducting continuous monitoring, and practicing vendor risk management, organizations can confidently embrace the cloud while safeguarding their valuable assets and sensitive data. A proactive approach to cloud security strengthens an organization's overall cybersecurity posture and empowers them to harness the benefits of the cloud securely.

B. Internet of Things (IoT) Security

The Internet of Things (IoT) has revolutionized the way we interact with technology, connecting various devices and systems to the internet for enhanced functionality and data exchange. While IoT offers tremendous benefits and convenience, it also introduces new cybersecurity challenges. IoT security is a crucial aspect of modern cybersecurity as organizations and individuals increasingly rely on interconnected devices. Safeguarding IoT devices is essential to prevent potential breaches, data theft, and unauthorized access.

Device Authentication and Identity Management

IoT devices must have robust authentication mechanisms to ensure that only authorized users can access them. Weak or default passwords are common entry points for cyber attackers. Implementing strong authentication methods such as unique credentials, certificates, or biometrics is vital to prevent unauthorized access to IoT devices.

Proper identity management practices help track and manage user identities, ensuring that only legitimate users can interact with IoT devices. This is particularly important in scenarios where multiple users or devices connect to the same IoT network.

Encryption of Data and Communication

IoT devices often collect and transmit sensitive data. Securing data in transit and at rest is crucial to protect it from eavesdropping and tampering. Implementing end-to-end encryption ensures that data remains confidential, even if intercepted during transmission.

Encryption also applies to communication between IoT devices and cloud servers or gateways. Secure communication protocols, such as Transport Layer Security (TLS), prevent man-in-the-middle attacks and unauthorized access to IoT networks.

Regular Firmware Updates and Patch Management

Many IoT devices use firmware to operate, and vulnerabilities in firmware can be exploited by cyber attackers. Manufacturers must provide regular firmware updates and security patches to address known vulnerabilities and improve device security.

Similarly, IoT device users must promptly apply updates to ensure their devices remain protected against the latest threats. IoT devices should also support automatic updates to minimize the risk of unpatched vulnerabilities.

Secure Configuration and Default Settings

Default settings on IoT devices are often generic and not optimized for security. Manufacturers should encourage users to change default passwords, disable unnecessary features, and enable security settings during the initial setup.

Organizations and users must follow best practices for securely configuring IoT devices. This includes segmenting IoT devices on separate networks, restricting communication to only necessary ports and protocols, and disabling unused features to reduce the attack surface.

Monitoring and Anomaly Detection

Continuous monitoring of IoT devices is essential to detect abnormal behaviors or potential security breaches. Monitoring tools that analyze device activity can identify suspicious activities and alert administrators to take appropriate actions.

Implementing anomaly detection algorithms can help identify unusual patterns in IoT device behavior, such as unauthorized access attempts or data exfiltration. Early detection enables swift response and containment of potential threats.

Physical Security and Device Management

Physical security is a vital aspect of IoT security, especially for devices deployed in public spaces or industrial environments. Physical tampering or theft of IoT devices can compromise data and lead to unauthorized access.

Device management platforms help organizations centrally manage and secure a large number of IoT devices. These platforms enable device authentication, firmware updates, and security configurations at scale, simplifying the management and maintenance of IoT ecosystems.

In conclusion, IoT security is a critical consideration in the digital age. By implementing robust device authentication and identity management, encrypting data and communication, regularly updating firmware and patches, configuring devices securely, monitoring for anomalies, and ensuring physical security and centralized device management, organizations can enhance IoT security and reduce the risk of IoT-related cyber threats. As IoT continues to evolve and become more integrated into our lives and industries, a proactive approach to IoT security is essential to protect our interconnected world.

C. Mobile Device Security

Mobile devices have become an integral part of our daily lives, serving as communication tools, personal assistants, and gateways to the digital world. As the use of mobile devices continues to grow, so does the need for robust mobile device security. Mobile devices store sensitive information, access personal accounts, and connect to various networks, making them attractive targets for cyber attackers. Implementing effective mobile device security measures is essential to protect against mobile threats and ensure the confidentiality and integrity of data.

Device Authentication and Biometrics

Strong device authentication is the first line of defense in mobile device security. Devices should be protected by a secure passcode, PIN, pattern lock, or biometric authentication, such as fingerprint or facial recognition. These methods prevent unauthorized access to the device and safeguard sensitive information in case the device is lost or stolen.

Encryption for Data Protection

Enabling device encryption ensures that data stored on the mobile device is protected from unauthorized access, even if the device falls into the wrong hands. Encryption scrambles the data, and only the authorized user with the correct credentials can decrypt and access the data.

In addition to device-level encryption, communication between the mobile device and external servers should be encrypted using secure protocols such as HTTPS to protect data during transmission.

App Security and Permissions

Mobile apps pose security risks, especially if they are downloaded from untrusted sources. Organizations and users should only download apps from official app stores to minimize the risk of malware and malicious code.

App permissions should be carefully reviewed, and users should grant only the necessary permissions. Apps requesting excessive permissions can access sensitive data and compromise privacy and security.

Mobile Device Management (MDM)

For organizations managing a fleet of mobile devices, Mobile Device Management (MDM) solutions are crucial. MDM allows administrators to remotely manage and secure devices, enforce security policies, and remotely wipe data from lost or stolen devices.

MDM enables organizations to enforce password policies, control app installations, and enforce encryption on mobile devices used for business purposes, reducing the risk of data breaches and ensuring compliance with security standards.

Secure Wi-Fi and Network Connections

Public Wi-Fi networks can be vulnerable to cyber attacks. Connecting to unsecured Wi-Fi networks exposes mobile devices to risks like man-in-the-middle attacks, where attackers intercept data transmitted over the network.

Using virtual private networks (VPNs) on mobile devices adds an extra layer of security by encrypting traffic between the device and the VPN server, ensuring data privacy and security while using public Wi-Fi.

Regular Software Updates

Regularly updating the mobile device's operating system and apps is critical for mobile security. Software updates often include security patches that address known vulnerabilities and protect against the latest threats.

Enabling automatic updates ensures that devices receive the latest security fixes promptly, reducing the window of exposure to potential risks.

In conclusion, mobile device security is essential in the digital age to protect against cyber threats and safeguard sensitive data. By implementing strong device authentication, enabling encryption for data protection, being cautious with app security and permissions, using Mobile Device Management (MDM) solutions, connecting securely to Wi-Fi networks, and ensuring regular software updates, individuals and organizations can fortify their mobile devices against mobile threats. Mobile security practices should be an integral part of cybersecurity strategies, empowering users to enjoy the benefits of mobile technology while remaining vigilant about mobile security risks.

CHAPTER VII
Incident Response and Recovery

A. Preparing for Cyber Incidents

In today's cyber threat landscape, no organization is immune to cyber incidents. It is not a question of "if" but "when" a cyber incident will occur. Effective incident response and recovery planning are critical to minimize the impact of cyber attacks and swiftly restore normal operations. Preparing for cyber incidents involves proactive measures to strengthen an organization's ability to detect, respond, and recover from potential security breaches.

Establishing an Incident Response Team

Creating a dedicated incident response team is the first step in preparing for cyber incidents. This team should comprise skilled and trained professionals from various departments, including IT, cybersecurity, legal, communications, and management. The incident response team will be responsible for coordinating responses and actions during and after a cyber incident.

Developing an Incident Response Plan

An incident response plan is a comprehensive blueprint that outlines the steps to be taken in the event of a cyber incident. The plan should define roles and responsibilities, communication procedures, escalation paths, and technical actions to be executed during various types of incidents. It should also include a well-defined chain of command and incident categorization to prioritize responses based on the severity of the incident.

Conducting Tabletop Exercises

Tabletop exercises are simulated incident scenarios that allow the incident response team to practice their response procedures in a controlled environment. These exercises help identify gaps in the incident response plan, test communication channels, and improve coordination among team members. Regular tabletop exercises ensure that the team remains well-prepared and can respond effectively to real-world incidents.

Building Cyber Threat Intelligence

Cyber threat intelligence involves monitoring and analyzing potential threats and risks that may target the organization. Building a strong cyber threat intelligence program helps the incident response team stay informed about the latest attack trends, tactics, and techniques used by cyber adversaries. Threat intelligence allows organizations to proactively defend against potential threats and adjust their incident response strategies accordingly.

Implementing Real-Time Monitoring

Real-time monitoring of IT systems and networks is crucial for early detection of cyber incidents. Implementing Security Information and Event Management (SIEM) solutions and intrusion detection systems enables continuous monitoring of network traffic and system logs for suspicious activities. Prompt detection allows organizations to respond swiftly and mitigate potential damages.

Establishing Communication Protocols

Effective communication during a cyber incident is essential to keep all stakeholders informed and coordinate response efforts. Establishing communication protocols that define how and when to report incidents, whom to notify, and how to disseminate information internally and externally is critical. Open and transparent communication builds trust and minimizes the impact of a cyber incident on the organization's reputation.

Creating Backup and Recovery Strategies

Having comprehensive data backup and recovery strategies is crucial for restoring operations after a cyber incident. Regularly backing up critical data and storing it in secure, separate locations enables organizations to recover from ransomware attacks, data corruption, or other incidents with minimal data loss.

In conclusion, preparing for cyber incidents is essential for organizations to effectively respond to cyber threats and protect their assets and reputation. By establishing an incident response team, developing a comprehensive incident response plan, conducting tabletop exercises, building cyber threat intelligence, implementing real-time monitoring, establishing communication protocols, and creating backup and recovery strategies, organizations can proactively enhance their cyber resilience. A proactive approach to incident response and recovery empowers organizations to minimize the impact of cyber incidents and ensure business continuity in the face of evolving cyber threats.

B. Incident Identification and Classification

Effective incident response begins with timely and accurate identification and classification of cyber incidents. Incident identification involves recognizing potential security breaches and abnormal activities that could indicate malicious intent or unauthorized access. Once identified, incidents must be classified based on their severity and impact to prioritize response efforts and allocate resources effectively. A well-defined incident identification and classification process is essential for a swift and targeted response to cyber incidents.

Incident Identification

Incident identification relies on robust monitoring and detection mechanisms. Organizations should deploy advanced security tools and technologies, such as intrusion detection systems (IDS), security information and event management (SIEM), and endpoint detection and response (EDR) systems. These tools continuously monitor networks, systems, and endpoints for suspicious activities and potential security breaches.

Security personnel should also be vigilant in recognizing signs of possible incidents. Unusual network traffic patterns, unexpected system behavior, and suspicious user activities should all trigger further investigation.

Additionally, organizations can leverage threat intelligence feeds and information sharing platforms to stay informed about the latest cyber threats and indicators of compromise (IOCs). This knowledge can aid in the early detection of known threats and potential attacks.

Incident Classification

Incident classification involves categorizing identified incidents based on their severity, potential impact, and urgency of response. A common classification framework uses three broad categories:

a. High Severity Incidents: These incidents have a significant impact on the organization's operations, data, or reputation. They require immediate and intensive response efforts. Examples include large-scale data breaches, ransomware attacks, and system-wide disruptions.

b. Medium Severity Incidents: Incidents falling into this category have a moderate impact on the organization's operations and data. They require timely response and remediation. Examples include localized malware infections, phishing incidents, and unauthorized access to sensitive data.

c. Low Severity Incidents: Incidents in this category have minimal impact and can often be addressed with routine response procedures. They still require attention, but they may not demand immediate prioritization.

Examples include minor system vulnerabilities and unsuccessful intrusion attempts.

Classifying incidents also involves considering the potential risks associated with the incident. For instance, an incident involving a critical infrastructure component might be classified as high severity due to the potential for far-reaching consequences.

Incident Triage and Response

After incidents are classified, the incident response team performs triage to assess the situation further. Triage involves gathering additional information about the incident, determining the scope and affected assets, and verifying the classification. This process helps refine the incident response plan and define the appropriate actions to contain, eradicate, and recover from the incident.

Once triage is complete, the response team can implement the incident response plan, involving relevant stakeholders, coordinating actions, and ensuring timely communication with all necessary parties, including executives, IT staff, legal teams, and external authorities, if required.

In conclusion, incident identification and classification are fundamental stages in the incident response and recovery process. By implementing robust monitoring and detection mechanisms, leveraging threat intelligence, and promptly classifying incidents based on their severity and impact, organizations can respond swiftly and effectively to cyber incidents. Incident identification and classification lay the groundwork for a targeted and well-coordinated response, helping organizations minimize the impact of cyber threats and restore normal operations efficiently.

C. Mitigation and Recovery Strategies

When a cyber incident occurs, swift and effective mitigation and recovery strategies are essential to minimize the damage and restore normal operations. Incident response teams must act decisively to contain the incident, eradicate the threat, and recover affected systems and data. A well-prepared incident response plan with predefined mitigation and recovery strategies is crucial to efficiently navigate through a cyber incident.

Incident Mitigation

Mitigating the impact of a cyber incident involves taking immediate actions to stop the attack from spreading and causing further harm. Depending on the nature of the incident, mitigation strategies may include:

a. Isolation: Isolating affected systems or devices from the network can prevent the spread of malware or limit unauthorized access.

b. Disabling Compromised Accounts: Disabling compromised user accounts or credentials can prevent unauthorized access and further misuse.

c. Blocking Malicious IP Addresses: Blocking known malicious IP addresses helps thwart ongoing attacks and prevents further communication with malicious actors.

d. Applying Security Patches: Quickly applying security patches and updates can close known vulnerabilities and prevent future exploitation.

e. Resetting Passwords: Requiring users to reset passwords after an incident helps ensure that compromised credentials are no longer usable.

Incident Eradication

Eradicating the threat involves removing all traces of the attacker's presence from the affected systems and network. This process may include:

a. Conducting a System Analysis: Investigating the affected systems and network to identify the source of the attack and understand the attacker's methods.

b. Removing Malware: Utilizing specialized anti-malware tools and manual investigation to locate and remove malicious code or files from affected systems.

c. Closing Exploitable Paths: Identifying and closing the vulnerabilities that allowed the attack to occur in the first place to prevent future similar incidents.

d. Conducting Root Cause Analysis: Analyzing the incident to understand its root cause and implementing measures to prevent similar incidents in the future.

Incident Recovery

The recovery phase focuses on restoring affected systems, services, and data to their normal state. Strategies for incident recovery may include:

a. Data Restoration: Restoring data from backups to recover any lost or encrypted data resulting from the incident.

b. System Rebuilds: Rebuilding compromised systems from clean installations and configurations to ensure their integrity.

c. Testing and Validation: Thoroughly testing and validating restored systems and data to ensure they are free from any lingering malicious elements.

d. Resuming Operations: Gradually resuming normal operations and services once the recovery is complete and validated.

Post-Incident Analysis and Lessons Learned

After the incident has been contained, eradicated, and recovery is complete, the incident response team conducts a post-incident analysis. This analysis involves a comprehensive review of the incident response process, including strengths, weaknesses, and lessons learned. The insights gained from this analysis contribute to improving future incident response plans and enhancing overall cybersecurity measures.

In conclusion, having well-defined mitigation and recovery strategies is essential for effective incident response and recovery. Incident response teams must act swiftly to contain and eradicate the threat while focusing on a methodical recovery process to restore normal operations. By combining immediate mitigation actions, thorough eradication efforts, and meticulous recovery procedures, organizations can navigate through cyber incidents with resilience and ensure business continuity. Furthermore, the post-incident analysis enables continuous improvement, making future incident response efforts more efficient and robust.

CHAPTER VIII
Beyond the Basics: Advanced Cybersecurity Strategies

A. Threat Hunting and Cyber Threat Intelligence

As cyber threats continue to evolve in sophistication and complexity, organizations must move beyond traditional cybersecurity measures to stay ahead of adversaries. Advanced cybersecurity strategies, such as threat hunting and cyber threat intelligence, play a vital role in proactively identifying and mitigating cyber threats before they cause significant damage. These strategies empower organizations to be more proactive, adaptive, and effective in their defense against cyber threats.

Threat Hunting

Threat hunting is a proactive approach to cybersecurity that involves actively searching for hidden threats and potential security breaches within an organization's network and systems. Unlike traditional cybersecurity measures that rely on automated security tools and alerts, threat hunting leverages human expertise and intuition to identify threats that may have evaded detection.

Threat hunters, often highly skilled cybersecurity professionals, use a combination of data analytics, log analysis, behavioral analysis, and threat intelligence to search for signs of malicious activities. They look for anomalies, patterns, and indicators of compromise (IOCs) that may indicate the presence of advanced and stealthy threats.

By engaging in threat hunting, organizations can detect and respond to threats at an early stage, before they escalate into full-blown security incidents. This proactive approach helps prevent data breaches, minimize damages, and protect critical assets and information.

Cyber Threat Intelligence (CTI)

Cyber Threat Intelligence (CTI) involves gathering, analyzing, and sharing information about cyber threats and adversaries. CTI provides organizations with contextualized and actionable insights into the tactics, techniques, and procedures (TTPs) used by cyber adversaries.

There are two main types of CTI:

a. Strategic CTI: Strategic CTI focuses on the long-term understanding of threat actors, their motives, and the overall cyber threat landscape. It helps organizations assess their risk exposure and develop proactive cybersecurity strategies.

b. Tactical CTI: Tactical CTI provides real-time and technical details about specific threats and vulnerabilities. It helps incident response teams and security operations center (SOC) analysts understand the latest attack trends and adapt their defenses accordingly.

By leveraging CTI, organizations can proactively identify emerging threats, anticipate cyber attacks, and strengthen their security posture. CTI also enables organizations to share threat intelligence with other trusted entities, fostering a collaborative and collective defense against cyber threats.

Integrating Threat Hunting and CTI

Combining threat hunting with CTI creates a powerful synergy that enhances an organization's ability to detect and respond to advanced cyber threats. Threat hunters can use cyber threat intelligence to focus their hunting efforts on the most relevant and prevalent threats.

CTI enriches the data used in threat hunting, providing valuable context and adversary behavior patterns that may not be immediately evident from internal data sources alone. This integration enables organizations to identify threats faster, understand their tactics, and take targeted and effective measures to mitigate risks.

Furthermore, the knowledge gained from threat hunting can be fed back into CTI efforts, improving the organization's overall cyber threat intelligence and helping refine and expand proactive cybersecurity strategies.

In conclusion, advanced cybersecurity strategies such as threat hunting and cyber threat intelligence are critical for staying ahead of cyber adversaries in today's evolving threat landscape. By engaging in proactive threat hunting and leveraging cyber threat intelligence, organizations can detect and respond to threats at an early stage, strengthen their cybersecurity posture, and collaborate with others in the cybersecurity community. Embracing these advanced strategies empowers organizations to be more resilient, adaptive, and capable of defending against emerging cyber threats.

B. Dealing with Nation-State and Advanced Persistent Threats

Nation-state actors and advanced persistent threats (APTs) represent some of the most formidable and sophisticated adversaries in the cybersecurity landscape. These attackers are often well-funded, possess advanced capabilities, and have significant resources at their disposal. Dealing with nation-state and APT threats requires a multifaceted and adaptive approach that goes beyond traditional cybersecurity measures.

Understand the Threat Landscape

To effectively counter nation-state and APT threats, organizations must gain a comprehensive understanding of the threat landscape. This involves studying the tactics, techniques, and procedures (TTPs) employed by these adversaries and analyzing their motivations and targets. Additionally, staying abreast of geopolitical events and regional cyber activities can provide valuable insights into potential threats.

Advanced Threat Detection and Response

Standard cybersecurity tools may not be sufficient to detect and respond to nation-state and APT attacks. Advanced threat detection solutions, such as behavior-based analytics, anomaly detection, and machine learning, are essential for identifying subtle and sophisticated attack patterns.

Security operations centers (SOCs) play a crucial role in monitoring and responding to advanced threats. SOC analysts, equipped with advanced tools and expertise, continuously monitor network traffic, analyze logs, and investigate potential security incidents to identify and neutralize emerging threats.

Threat Intelligence Sharing

Collaboration and threat intelligence sharing within the cybersecurity community are essential when dealing with nation-state and APT threats. By sharing threat intelligence with other organizations, government agencies, and industry partners, collective defense efforts can be strengthened. Trusted partnerships facilitate the exchange of valuable insights, enabling early detection and proactive measures against shared adversaries.

Zero Trust Architecture

A Zero Trust architecture is increasingly considered a best practice to protect against APTs and nation-state attacks. In a Zero Trust model, all network traffic, even from inside the organization's network, is treated as potentially malicious. This approach requires strict identity verification, continuous monitoring, and strong access controls to limit lateral movement within the network.

Endpoint Protection and EDR

Endpoints are frequent targets of APTs and nation-state actors. Advanced endpoint protection solutions, coupled with Endpoint Detection and Response (EDR) capabilities, provide organizations with real-time visibility into endpoint activities and swift response to any suspicious behavior. EDR can aid in identifying and containing APT attacks at the earliest stages.

Cybersecurity Awareness and Training

Human factors are often exploited by APTs for initial access. Raising cybersecurity awareness among employees and conducting regular training can reduce the risk of falling victim to social engineering and phishing attacks. Employees should be educated about the significance of cybersecurity best practices and the potential impact of their actions on the organization's security posture.

Incident Simulation and Red Teaming

Conducting incident simulations and red teaming exercises allows organizations to test their response capabilities against simulated nation-state and APT attacks. These exercises help identify weaknesses in the incident response process and provide valuable insights into areas that require improvement.

In conclusion, dealing with nation-state and advanced persistent threats requires a proactive and comprehensive approach. By understanding the threat landscape, deploying advanced threat detection and response mechanisms, sharing threat intelligence, adopting a Zero Trust architecture, implementing robust endpoint protection and EDR, prioritizing cybersecurity awareness and training, and conducting incident simulations and red teaming, organizations can enhance their resilience against these sophisticated adversaries. Combining advanced cybersecurity strategies with a vigilant and well-prepared cybersecurity workforce enables organizations to stand firm against nation-state and APT threats and protect their critical assets and sensitive information from being compromised.

C. Artificial Intelligence and Machine Learning in Cybersecurity

As cyber threats become more sophisticated and pervasive, the cybersecurity landscape demands innovative solutions to counter the ever-evolving risks. Artificial Intelligence (AI) and Machine Learning (ML) have emerged as game-changing technologies in the field of cybersecurity. By leveraging the power of AI and ML, organizations can significantly enhance their ability to detect, prevent, and respond to cyber threats with greater speed and accuracy.

Threat Detection and Analysis

AI and ML are particularly effective in threat detection and analysis. These technologies can process vast amounts of data, including network traffic, logs, and user behavior, to identify patterns and anomalies indicative of malicious activities. ML algorithms can recognize new and previously unseen threats, enabling proactive defense against zero-day attacks and advanced persistent threats (APTs).

By continuously learning from new data and adapting to changing attack patterns, AI-powered threat detection systems can significantly reduce false positives and false negatives, ensuring efficient and accurate identification of potential security incidents.

Behavior-Based Authentication

Traditional authentication methods based on static credentials are increasingly vulnerable to cyberattacks, such as credential stuffing and brute-force attacks. AI and ML enable behavior-based authentication, where a user's typical behavior is analyzed to determine if access attempts are legitimate or potentially malicious.

This dynamic authentication process assesses various factors, such as location, device, and user behavior, to make real-time decisions about granting access. This way, AI and ML contribute to stronger user authentication and reduce the risk of unauthorized access.

Advanced Malware Detection

AI and ML play a critical role in advanced malware detection. AI-powered antivirus and endpoint security solutions can recognize malware patterns, even if the malware has mutated or used sophisticated obfuscation techniques. Additionally, ML algorithms can identify malware behavior in real-time, enabling swift responses to malware outbreaks.

Automated Incident Response

AI and ML facilitate automated incident response, where security incidents are detected, analyzed, and addressed with minimal human intervention. Automated incident response can contain threats in their early stages, preventing potential damages and reducing response time.

For instance, AI can automatically quarantine infected endpoints or block malicious IP addresses as soon as suspicious activities are detected, limiting the impact of an ongoing attack.

Predictive Security Analytics

AI and ML enable predictive security analytics, where historical data and ongoing threat intelligence are analyzed to forecast potential cyber threats and vulnerabilities. Predictive analytics empower organizations to prioritize security measures based on the likelihood of specific threats, improving resource allocation and decision-making.

Adaptive Access Controls

AI and ML enhance access control mechanisms by continuously monitoring user behavior and adjusting access privileges accordingly. For example, if an AI system detects unusual behavior from a normally trusted user, it may automatically reduce the user's access permissions to prevent potential data breaches.

In conclusion, the integration of AI and ML into cybersecurity strategies is a powerful advancement in the battle against cyber threats. By utilizing these technologies for threat detection and analysis, behavior-based authentication, advanced malware detection, automated incident response, predictive security analytics, and adaptive access controls, organizations can significantly bolster their cybersecurity defenses.

However, it is important to note that AI and ML are not a silver bullet, and human expertise remains vital in interpreting and fine-tuning the output of these technologies. Organizations should continue to invest in skilled cybersecurity professionals, while also harnessing the transformative potential of AI and ML to build a more resilient and proactive cybersecurity posture. Combining human intelligence with AI-powered technologies empowers organizations to stay ahead of cyber threats and safeguard their valuable assets in an increasingly complex digital landscape.

CHAPTER IX
Securing Emerging Technologies

A. Blockchain Security

Blockchain technology has gained immense popularity in recent years, revolutionizing various industries by providing decentralized and tamper-resistant data storage and transaction mechanisms. However, like any emerging technology, blockchain is not immune to security challenges. Securing blockchain networks and applications is essential to ensure the integrity, confidentiality, and availability of data and transactions within the blockchain ecosystem.

Consensus Mechanism Security

Blockchain networks rely on consensus mechanisms to validate and agree on the state of the ledger across multiple nodes. Common consensus mechanisms include Proof of Work (PoW) and Proof of Stake (PoS). Securing these mechanisms is critical to prevent attacks, such as 51% attacks in PoW networks or stake grinding in PoS networks.

Implementing robust consensus protocols and continuously monitoring network activity can help detect and mitigate potential threats to the blockchain's security.

Smart Contract Auditing

Smart contracts are self-executing pieces of code that facilitate transactions and automate processes within a blockchain. Smart contract vulnerabilities can lead to catastrophic consequences, as they are immutable once deployed.

Thoroughly auditing smart contracts before deployment is essential to identify and address potential security flaws. Formal verification techniques and third-party security audits can help ensure the reliability and safety of smart contracts.

Private Key Management

Blockchain users rely on cryptographic keys to access and sign transactions. Proper private key management is crucial to prevent unauthorized access to users' accounts and assets.

Using hardware wallets, secure key vaults, or multi-signature solutions can enhance private key security and reduce the risk of theft or compromise.

Permissioned Blockchains

While public blockchains are open to anyone, permissioned blockchains restrict access to authorized participants. Organizations may choose permissioned blockchains to control data visibility and network governance.

Securing permissioned blockchains involves carefully managing user access, identity verification, and participant onboarding procedures.

Network Security

Like any distributed system, blockchain networks are susceptible to Distributed Denial of Service (DDoS) attacks and other network-level threats. Implementing robust network security measures, such as firewalls, intrusion detection systems, and load balancers, can help protect blockchain nodes from such attacks.

Regular Software Updates

Blockchain networks and platforms are constantly evolving, with developers releasing updates to address security vulnerabilities and enhance functionality. Regularly updating blockchain software and applications is vital to stay ahead of potential threats and ensure the latest security patches are applied.

Decentralization and Attack Surface

Blockchain networks' decentralization is a double-edged sword. While it enhances resilience by eliminating central points of failure, it also creates a broader attack surface.

Organizations must be vigilant in monitoring and securing the various nodes and participants in the blockchain network. Encouraging network participation from diverse entities can strengthen the network's decentralization and security.

In conclusion, securing blockchain technology is crucial to unleash its full potential as a transformative and secure platform for various applications. By focusing on consensus mechanism security, smart contract auditing, private key management, permissioned blockchains, network security, regular software updates, and decentralization, organizations can enhance the security of their blockchain networks. As blockchain continues to evolve and integrate into more industries, a proactive and comprehensive approach to blockchain security is vital for building trust and confidence in the technology's capabilities and fostering widespread adoption.

B. Quantum Computing and Its Implications

Quantum computing is an emerging technology that has the potential to revolutionize computing as we know it. Unlike classical computers that use bits to represent information as 0s and 1s, quantum computers use quantum bits or qubits, which can exist in multiple states simultaneously, thanks to the principles of quantum mechanics. This enables quantum computers to perform complex calculations exponentially faster than classical computers for certain types of problems.

While quantum computing offers exciting possibilities for solving complex scientific and computational challenges, it also poses significant implications for cybersecurity and data security.

Cryptography and Encryption

One of the most significant implications of quantum computing is its potential to break widely used encryption algorithms that secure our digital communications and data. Many of the cryptographic protocols used today, such as RSA and ECC (Elliptic Curve Cryptography), rely on the difficulty of factoring large numbers or solving certain mathematical problems, which are currently beyond the reach of classical computers.

However, quantum computers could theoretically perform these calculations efficiently using Shor's algorithm, rendering conventional cryptographic methods vulnerable. This raises concerns about the security of sensitive data and communications once large-scale quantum computers become a reality.

Post-Quantum Cryptography

To address the threat posed by quantum computing to traditional encryption methods, researchers are actively working on post-quantum cryptography. These are cryptographic algorithms and protocols specifically designed to be resistant to quantum attacks.

Post-quantum cryptography explores mathematical problems that are believed to be hard even for quantum computers, ensuring that encrypted data remains secure even in the face of quantum threats. Migrating to post-quantum cryptographic standards will be essential to safeguard sensitive information in a quantum-powered world.

Quantum Key Distribution

Quantum computing also offers a solution to quantum-safe key distribution through quantum key distribution (QKD) protocols. QKD leverages the principles of quantum mechanics to generate and distribute encryption keys that are theoretically unbreakable, even by a quantum computer.

QKD ensures that secure keys can be exchanged between parties without the risk of interception or eavesdropping. This technology has the potential to provide a secure foundation for communication in a quantum computing era.

Breakthroughs in Cryptanalysis

Quantum computing's immense computational power could potentially lead to breakthroughs in cryptanalysis. While quantum computers can threaten existing encryption methods, they may also facilitate the development of more efficient cryptanalysis techniques to crack encrypted data.

This emphasizes the need for continuous research and development in both quantum-resistant encryption and quantum-safe cryptanalysis.

Accelerating Scientific Discoveries

On a positive note, quantum computing can accelerate scientific discoveries in fields like chemistry, materials science, drug design, and optimization problems. Quantum simulations could help solve complex scientific challenges that are infeasible for classical computers.

As quantum computing advances, it will revolutionize industries and scientific research, providing new opportunities for innovation and problem-solving.

In conclusion, quantum computing is a transformative technology with profound implications for cybersecurity and data security. While it holds tremendous potential to solve complex problems and fuel scientific advancements, it also challenges the existing cryptographic foundations that protect our digital world.

To secure emerging technologies like quantum computing, a multi-faceted approach is necessary. This includes exploring post-quantum cryptographic standards, adopting quantum key distribution for secure key exchange, investing in quantum-safe cryptanalysis research, and preparing for the era of quantum computing with forward-thinking cybersecurity strategies. By staying proactive and adaptive, we can harness the power of quantum computing while safeguarding the confidentiality, integrity, and availability of sensitive information in a quantum-powered future.

C. Augmented Reality and Virtual Reality Security

Augmented Reality (AR) and Virtual Reality (VR) are immersive technologies that have gained significant traction in various industries, including gaming, entertainment, education, and healthcare. AR enhances the real-world environment by overlaying digital content, while VR creates entirely virtual environments for users to explore. While these technologies offer exciting possibilities, they also introduce new security challenges that must be addressed to ensure user safety and data integrity.

Privacy Concerns

AR and VR applications often collect extensive user data to provide personalized and immersive experiences. This data may include user interactions, physical movements, voice inputs, and even biometric information. Ensuring user privacy is essential, and developers must implement robust data protection measures to safeguard sensitive information.

Compliance with privacy regulations, such as the General Data Protection Regulation (GDPR), is crucial to prevent unauthorized access or misuse of user data.

Authentication and Authorization

AR and VR systems may incorporate user authentication features to grant access to specific features or content. Ensuring strong authentication and authorization mechanisms is essential to prevent unauthorized users from accessing sensitive information or participating in potentially harmful activities.

Multi-factor authentication, biometric recognition, and role-based access controls are some of the measures that can enhance the security of AR and VR applications.

Secure Data Transmission

In AR and VR applications, data may be transmitted between the user's device and remote servers for processing and rendering. Securing data transmission through encryption protocols, such as TLS/SSL, is crucial to prevent eavesdropping and man-in-the-middle attacks.

Additionally, developers should consider minimizing the amount of data transmitted and stored to reduce the risk of data exposure.

Content Security

AR and VR applications rely heavily on digital content, such as 3D models, textures, and audio files. Ensuring the authenticity and integrity of this content is vital to prevent malicious content injection or tampering.

Digital signatures and content verification mechanisms can help ensure that content comes from trusted sources and has not been altered during transmission.

Device Security

AR and VR applications often run on a variety of devices, including smartphones, headsets, and other wearables. Securing these devices against unauthorized access, malware, and exploitation is essential to prevent potential threats.

Developers should follow security best practices for app development and regularly update applications to address known vulnerabilities.

Social Engineering and Cyber Attacks

As AR and VR technologies become more popular, they may also become targets for social engineering and cyber attacks. Users may be exposed to phishing attempts, fake AR/VR content, or malware disguised as legitimate applications.

Raising awareness about these risks through user education and implementing security features to identify and block malicious content can help mitigate these threats.

In conclusion, securing augmented reality and virtual reality technologies is paramount to protect user privacy, data integrity, and overall user safety. By addressing privacy concerns, implementing strong authentication and authorization mechanisms, securing data transmission, ensuring content authenticity, enhancing device security, and mitigating social engineering and cyber attacks, developers can create a safer and more trustworthy AR and VR experience.

Collaboration between technology providers, industry stakeholders, and cybersecurity experts is essential to develop comprehensive security frameworks that enable the widespread adoption of AR and VR while safeguarding users from potential risks and threats. Embracing emerging technologies with a security-first mindset is crucial to unlocking their full potential and ensuring a positive and secure user experience.

CHAPTER X
The Future of Cybersecurity

A. Anticipating Future Threats and Challenges

The future of cybersecurity holds both promises and challenges, as technology continues to advance at a rapid pace. As organizations embrace digital transformation and emerging technologies, they must also be prepared to face new and sophisticated cyber threats. Anticipating these future threats and challenges is crucial to stay ahead of cyber adversaries and ensure a secure and resilient cyber landscape.

Artificial Intelligence and Machine Learning-Driven Attacks

As AI and ML technologies become more prevalent in various domains, cybercriminals are also expected to leverage these advanced tools for orchestrating attacks. AI-driven attacks have the potential to bypass traditional security defenses by adapting and evolving in real-time.

Anticipating AI-driven threats requires the development of AI-based cybersecurity solutions capable of detecting and countering AI-generated attacks. The cybersecurity community must invest in AI and ML research to create robust defenses that can outsmart cyber adversaries.

Quantum Threats

The advent of practical quantum computers poses a significant challenge to traditional cryptographic algorithms, which could be easily broken using quantum algorithms. As quantum computing evolves, organizations must transition to quantum-resistant encryption methods to safeguard sensitive data and communications.

Research into quantum-safe cryptographic techniques and the implementation of quantum-resistant protocols are vital to preparing for the quantum threat landscape.

Internet of Things (IoT) Vulnerabilities

The proliferation of IoT devices in homes, businesses, and critical infrastructures expands the attack surface for cybercriminals. Insecure IoT devices are often vulnerable to exploitation, leading to data breaches, network compromise, and even physical harm in the case of critical infrastructure.

Anticipating future IoT vulnerabilities necessitates improved IoT security standards, regular software updates, and the establishment of a secure IoT ecosystem where device manufacturers, service providers, and end-users collaborate to ensure device security.

Supply Chain Attacks

Supply chain attacks have become increasingly sophisticated, targeting software and hardware vendors to compromise products before reaching end-users. Such attacks can have cascading effects on a wide range of organizations relying on these compromised products.

To anticipate future supply chain attacks, organizations must enhance supply chain risk management, perform thorough security assessments of vendors, and implement measures to verify the integrity of software and hardware throughout the supply chain.

Ransomware Evolution

Ransomware attacks have evolved into highly lucrative and targeted operations, with cybercriminals demanding substantial ransoms from organizations to unlock their encrypted data. Future ransomware attacks are likely to involve more sophisticated encryption techniques and advanced evasion mechanisms.

To anticipate ransomware evolution, organizations should focus on data backup strategies, network segmentation, and user training to mitigate the impact of ransomware attacks.

Convergence of Physical and Cyber Threats

With the rise of smart cities, industrial IoT, and interconnected systems, the convergence of physical and cyber threats becomes a significant concern. Cyberattacks that target critical infrastructures, such as power grids or transportation networks, can have severe real-world consequences.

Anticipating this convergence requires collaboration between cybersecurity professionals, physical security experts, and policymakers to develop comprehensive strategies that protect both cyber and physical domains.

In conclusion, anticipating future threats and challenges in cybersecurity is essential to prepare for the rapidly changing cyber landscape. Embracing emerging technologies while proactively addressing potential vulnerabilities and risks is crucial for organizations and individuals alike. The future of cybersecurity will require continuous innovation, collaboration, and a strong commitment to building a secure digital ecosystem. By staying vigilant, adaptive, and investing in cutting-edge research, the cybersecurity community can stay ahead of cyber threats and create a safer and more secure digital future for all.

B. The Role of Governments and International Cooperation

In the ever-evolving landscape of cybersecurity, governments and international cooperation play a crucial role in shaping policies, strategies, and responses to cyber threats. As cybercriminals and nation-state actors continue to exploit digital vulnerabilities, a coordinated and collaborative approach among nations becomes essential to establish a secure and resilient global cyberspace.

Formulating Cybersecurity Policies and Regulations

Governments play a central role in formulating cybersecurity policies and regulations that set the framework for protecting critical infrastructure, businesses, and citizens. Effective cybersecurity policies involve risk assessments, data protection guidelines, incident response protocols, and measures to address emerging threats.

International cooperation is vital in sharing best practices and knowledge to develop robust policies that align with global cybersecurity goals.

Strengthening Legal Frameworks

The enactment and enforcement of cybercrime laws are essential to deter cybercriminals and hold them accountable for their actions. Governments must collaborate to establish legal frameworks that enable the prosecution of cybercriminals across borders.

Mutual legal assistance treaties and extradition agreements facilitate cooperation in investigating and prosecuting cybercriminals who operate internationally.

Sharing Cyber Threat Intelligence

Cyber threat intelligence sharing between governments and international organizations enhance collective defense against cyber threats. Timely exchange of information about emerging threats, malware samples, and attack patterns enables faster and more effective responses to cyber incidents.

Collaboration through information-sharing platforms fosters a proactive approach to cybersecurity, benefiting all participating nations.

Promoting Capacity Building and Awareness

Governments can promote cybersecurity capacity building by investing in education, training, and research in the field of cybersecurity. By empowering cybersecurity professionals and creating a skilled workforce, nations can enhance their ability to combat cyber threats.

Raising cybersecurity awareness among citizens and businesses is equally important. Governments can drive awareness campaigns that educate the public about cyber risks and best practices to stay safe online.

Diplomatic Efforts in Cyberspace

International cooperation in cyberspace requires diplomatic efforts to address cyber incidents and conflicts responsibly. Governments should engage in open dialogues to deescalate tensions arising from cyber activities and establish norms of responsible behavior in cyberspace.

International organizations, such as the United Nations and the International Telecommunication Union (ITU), can serve as platforms for multilateral discussions on cyber norms and cooperation.

Establishing Cyber Incident Response Mechanisms

Collaborative cyber incident response mechanisms are essential to coordinate actions and share resources during large-scale cyber incidents. Governments can establish cyber response teams and networks to facilitate information exchange and support each other in mitigating cyber threats.

Coordinated responses enable a unified approach, preventing cyber incidents from escalating into larger-scale crises.

In conclusion, as the future of cybersecurity unfolds, governments and international cooperation will be instrumental in fostering a secure and trustworthy cyberspace. By formulating effective cybersecurity policies, strengthening legal frameworks, sharing cyber threat intelligence, promoting capacity building and awareness, engaging in diplomatic efforts, and establishing cyber incident response mechanisms, nations can collectively address the challenges posed by cyber threats.

Cybersecurity is a global challenge that requires global solutions. The synergy of governments, international organizations, private sectors, and individuals working together will be the cornerstone of a secure digital future. With strong international cooperation and a commitment to cybersecurity, nations can forge a path towards a safer and more resilient cyber ecosystem for the benefit of all.

C. Ethical Considerations in Cybersecurity

As technology continues to shape the future of cybersecurity, ethical considerations take on increased importance in ensuring that cybersecurity practices align with moral principles and human values. Cybersecurity professionals and policymakers must navigate complex ethical dilemmas to strike a balance between security needs and protecting individual rights and privacy. As the cyber landscape evolves, several key ethical considerations emerge:

Privacy and Data Protection

Protecting individual privacy and data is paramount in the digital age. Cybersecurity measures must respect user consent and transparency when collecting, processing, and storing personal information. Striking the right balance between data security and data privacy is essential to avoid unnecessary intrusions into individuals' lives while safeguarding them from cyber threats.

Ethical cybersecurity practices involve implementing robust encryption, data anonymization, and data minimization techniques to ensure that data is protected from unauthorized access and use.

Responsible Vulnerability Disclosure

Discovering vulnerabilities in software and systems is an essential part of cybersecurity research. However, disclosing vulnerabilities responsibly is crucial to prevent malicious exploitation.

Ethical hackers and researchers should follow established disclosure guidelines, notifying the relevant vendors or organizations before making vulnerabilities public. This allows time for patching and mitigating potential risks, reducing harm to users and organizations.

Bias and Fairness in AI Security

As AI and machine learning technologies become integral to cybersecurity, ensuring fairness and mitigating bias are critical. Biases in AI algorithms can lead to discriminatory outcomes and negatively impact individuals and communities.

Ethical considerations involve auditing AI models for biases, ensuring diverse representation in training data, and being transparent about the limitations and potential biases of AI-driven security solutions.

Cyber Weapon Proliferation

The development and use of cyber weapons raise ethical questions about their potential impact on global security and civilian populations. Cybersecurity practitioners and policymakers must grapple with ethical dilemmas surrounding the development, deployment, and use of offensive cyber capabilities.

Ensuring accountability, transparency, and international norms in cyber warfare can help mitigate the risks associated with cyber weapon proliferation.

Balancing Security and Civil Liberties

In the pursuit of robust cybersecurity, there may be instances where security measures clash with civil liberties, such as freedom of speech, expression, and privacy. Striking the right balance is essential to avoid unnecessary intrusion into individual freedoms while safeguarding against cyber threats.

Ethical cybersecurity practices require transparency in surveillance and data collection, with oversight mechanisms to ensure that security measures do not infringe upon civil liberties.

Cybersecurity Workforce Ethics

Cybersecurity professionals must adhere to ethical standards in their work, particularly when dealing with sensitive data and cyber investigations. Upholding professional ethics includes respecting client confidentiality, refraining from unauthorized access or misuse of information, and maintaining integrity in reporting findings.

Cybersecurity practitioners must also be cautious of conflicts of interest and prioritize the greater good over personal gain.

In conclusion, ethical considerations are integral to the future of cybersecurity. As technology advances and cyber threats evolve, adhering to ethical principles is crucial in building a secure and trustworthy cyber ecosystem. Privacy and data protection, responsible vulnerability disclosure, fairness in AI security, cyber weapon proliferation, balancing security and civil liberties, and maintaining workforce ethics are all critical aspects of ethical cybersecurity practices.

By embracing ethical considerations, cybersecurity professionals and policymakers can ensure that cybersecurity measures protect individuals, organizations, and societies while upholding moral values and human rights. Ethical cybersecurity practices are the foundation for a future where technology and security work harmoniously to create a safer and more resilient digital world.

CHAPTER XI
Developing a Personal Cybersecurity Mindset

A. Practicing Good Cyber Hygiene

In an increasingly digital world, developing a personal cybersecurity mindset is essential to safeguarding our digital identities, sensitive information, and online activities. Practicing good cyber hygiene involves adopting proactive habits and behaviors that minimize the risk of falling victim to cyber threats and ensure a safe online experience. Here are some key elements of good cyber hygiene:

Strong and Unique Passwords

Using strong and unique passwords for all online accounts is a fundamental aspect of cyber hygiene. Passwords should be complex, containing a mix of uppercase and lowercase letters, numbers, and special characters. Avoid using easily guessable information, such as birthdates or names, and never reuse passwords across multiple accounts.

Consider using password managers to securely store and manage passwords, reducing the burden of memorizing numerous complex combinations.

Two-Factor Authentication (2FA)

Enabling two-factor authentication whenever possible adds an extra layer of security to online accounts. 2FA requires users to provide an additional verification code or a biometric factor, such as a fingerprint, along with their password to access an account. This significantly reduces the risk of unauthorized access, even if the password is compromised.

Regular Software Updates

Keeping software, operating systems, and applications up to date is crucial for addressing known security vulnerabilities. Cybercriminals often exploit outdated software to gain access to systems and steal sensitive data.

Enable automatic updates whenever possible, or regularly check for updates and apply them promptly to ensure optimal security.

Secure Wi-Fi Usage

When using public Wi-Fi networks, exercise caution to avoid potential security risks. Public Wi-Fi is often unsecured, making it vulnerable to eavesdropping and data interception.

Avoid accessing sensitive accounts or sharing personal information while on public Wi-Fi. Consider using a virtual private network (VPN) for an additional layer of encryption and protection.

Be Cautious with Email and Links

Phishing attacks continue to be a prevalent method used by cybercriminals to deceive users into revealing sensitive information. Be cautious with email attachments and links, especially from unknown or suspicious sources.

Avoid clicking on links in emails unless you are confident about their legitimacy. Verify the sender's email address and look for signs of phishing, such as spelling errors or requests for personal information.

Secure Social Media Practices

Be mindful of the information you share on social media platforms. Oversharing personal details can provide cybercriminals with valuable information for social engineering attacks.

Adjust privacy settings on social media accounts to control who can view your posts and limit access to personal information.

Regular Backups

Regularly backing up important data is an essential part of cyber hygiene. In the event of a ransomware attack or data loss incident, having recent backups ensures you can recover your data without paying a ransom.

Use external hard drives or cloud storage solutions for backups and ensure that they are securely encrypted.

In conclusion, practicing good cyber hygiene is a fundamental step in developing a personal cybersecurity mindset. By adopting strong and unique passwords, enabling two-factor authentication, keeping software updated, using secure Wi-Fi connections, being cautious with email and links, securing social media practices, and regularly backing up data, individuals can significantly reduce their risk of falling victim to cyber threats.

Developing a personal cybersecurity mindset is an ongoing process that requires vigilance, education, and a commitment to staying informed about the latest cybersecurity best practices. By incorporating these habits into our daily online activities, we can create a safer digital environment for ourselves and contribute to a more secure cyberspace for everyone.

B. Balancing Convenience and Security

In the digital age, the challenge of balancing convenience with security is a critical aspect of developing a personal cybersecurity mindset. As technology continues to integrate into every aspect of our lives, striking the right balance between easy access to digital services and protecting our sensitive information becomes essential. While convenience enhances our online experiences, it should never come at the expense of compromising security. Here are some key considerations for finding the right balance:

Password Management

One of the most significant challenges in balancing convenience and security is managing passwords. While it is tempting to use simple and easily memorable passwords for the sake of convenience, this approach compromises security. On the other hand, setting highly complex and unique passwords for each account can become cumbersome and challenging to remember.

Using password managers can help strike a balance between convenience and security. These tools generate strong, unique passwords for each account and store them securely, requiring users to remember only one master password.

Two-Factor Authentication (2FA)

Enabling two-factor authentication (2FA) is an excellent way to enhance security without sacrificing much convenience. 2FA provides an additional layer of protection by requiring a second verification step, such as a code sent to a mobile device, after entering the password.

By opting for 2FA whenever possible, users add an extra security measure without significantly disrupting their usual login process.

Biometric Authentication

Biometric authentication, such as fingerprint or facial recognition, offers a convenient and secure alternative to traditional passwords. These methods provide quick and seamless access to devices or applications while enhancing security through unique biological markers.

Using biometric authentication strikes a balance between convenience and security, as users do not need to remember passwords, and the system remains highly resistant to unauthorized access.

App Permissions

Mobile apps often request access to various device functions and personal data. While granting these permissions might enhance the app's functionality, it can also compromise user privacy and security.

Finding the balance between granting necessary permissions for app functionality and protecting personal data involves carefully reviewing app permissions and only allowing access to what is genuinely required.

Public Wi-Fi Usage

Public Wi-Fi networks are convenient for staying connected on the go, but they are also risky due to potential security vulnerabilities. Avoiding sensitive transactions, such as online banking, while on public Wi-Fi networks is a prudent security measure.

By being mindful of the risks and using a virtual private network (VPN) for added security, users can enjoy the convenience of public Wi-Fi while protecting their data.

Regular Updates

Updating software and applications regularly is essential for security, but it can be perceived as an inconvenience when updates disrupt workflow or require restarting devices.

Considering the potential security benefits and taking advantage of automatic updates whenever possible can help maintain the right balance between convenience and security.

In conclusion, finding the balance between convenience and security is an ongoing challenge in the digital age. By adopting password managers, enabling two-factor authentication, embracing biometric authentication, carefully managing app permissions, being cautious with public Wi-Fi usage, and prioritizing regular updates, individuals can achieve a balance that enhances their digital experiences while safeguarding their sensitive information.

A personal cybersecurity mindset involves making informed decisions that prioritize security without compromising everyday convenience. Striking this balance is essential for creating a safer and more enjoyable online environment, empowering users to take control of their digital lives responsibly.

C. Becoming an Active Cyber Citizen

In today's interconnected world, developing a personal cybersecurity mindset goes beyond protecting oneself; it extends to becoming an active cyber citizen. As technology continues to shape our daily lives, understanding the importance of responsible online behavior and contributing positively to the broader digital community becomes essential. Being an active cyber citizen means taking proactive steps to promote cybersecurity awareness, protect others from cyber threats, and contribute to a safer and more secure cyberspace for everyone. Here are some key aspects of becoming an active cyber citizen:

Cybersecurity Education and Awareness

Being an active cyber citizen begins with educating oneself about cybersecurity best practices and staying informed about the latest threats and trends. Regularly participating in cybersecurity awareness programs, webinars, and workshops can enhance knowledge and promote responsible digital behavior.

By sharing acquired knowledge with family, friends, and colleagues, active cyber citizens can empower others to protect themselves online.

Reporting Cyber Incidents

Reporting cyber incidents and suspicious activities to appropriate authorities is an essential aspect of being an active cyber citizen. Whether encountering phishing attempts, malware infections, or online scams, reporting these incidents helps authorities take necessary action and protect others from falling victim to similar threats.

Many governments and cybersecurity organizations have dedicated reporting portals for such incidents.

Engaging in Cyber Hygiene Advocacy

Promoting good cyber hygiene practices within one's social circles and community is an impactful way to become an active cyber citizen. Advocating for strong and unique passwords, two-factor authentication, and regular software updates can inspire positive change in the broader digital community.

Leading by example and encouraging others to adopt secure habits contribute to a collective improvement in cybersecurity.

Supporting Cybersecurity Initiatives

Actively supporting cybersecurity initiatives and organizations is another way to contribute to the digital community. Volunteering for cybersecurity awareness campaigns, supporting cybersecurity nonprofits, or participating in cybersecurity-related events can make a significant difference in raising awareness and driving positive change.

Encouraging Ethical Hacking and Bug Bounties

Ethical hacking and participating in bug bounty programs are avenues for active cyber citizens to use their cybersecurity skills responsibly. By helping organizations identify and fix vulnerabilities before malicious actors can exploit them, ethical hackers play a critical role in enhancing overall security.

Encouraging and supporting ethical hacking initiatives contributes to a safer digital environment for all.

Being Mindful of Online Conduct

Being an active cyber citizen involves being mindful of online conduct and engaging respectfully with others in digital spaces. Avoiding cyberbullying, hate speech, and other harmful behaviors creates a positive and inclusive online environment for everyone.

Cyber citizens should foster a culture of respect and empathy in digital interactions.

In conclusion, becoming an active cyber citizen is a commitment to not only personal cybersecurity but also to the collective well-being of the digital community. By investing in cybersecurity education, reporting incidents, advocating for cyber hygiene, supporting cybersecurity initiatives, encouraging ethical hacking, and promoting positive online conduct, individuals can contribute to a safer and more secure cyberspace for themselves and others.

Active cyber citizens are proactive in their approach to cybersecurity and recognize their role in building a digital environment that fosters trust, collaboration, and protection for all users. Embracing this mindset empowers individuals to make a positive impact and become responsible stewards of the digital world we share.

Conclusion

A. Embracing the Cybersecurity Mindset

In the fast-paced and digitally interconnected world we live in, embracing the cybersecurity mindset is no longer optional but imperative. Cyber threats continue to evolve, targeting individuals, businesses, governments, and critical infrastructures worldwide. To navigate this ever-changing landscape, it is essential for individuals to develop a cybersecurity mindset that prioritizes proactive measures, responsible behaviors, and continuous learning.

The journey to embracing the cybersecurity mindset begins with recognizing the significance of cybersecurity in our daily lives. Understanding that everyone is a potential target of cyber threats, regardless of technical expertise, is the first step toward taking personal responsibility for one's online security. Recognizing the impact of cyber incidents and data breaches on individuals and communities emphasizes the need for vigilance and precautionary measures.

Education is a cornerstone of the cybersecurity mindset. Staying informed about emerging threats, best practices, and evolving cybersecurity technologies empowers individuals to make informed decisions and adapt to changing circumstances. Cybersecurity education should be an ongoing process, where individuals actively seek knowledge and share it with their communities.

A critical aspect of the cybersecurity mindset is proactive risk management. This involves implementing strong security measures, such as using complex and unique passwords, enabling multi-factor authentication, and keeping software up to date. By taking proactive steps, individuals can significantly reduce their vulnerability to cyber threats and potential data breaches.

The cybersecurity mindset extends beyond personal protection to collective responsibility. As active cyber citizens, individuals play a crucial role in contributing positively to the broader digital community. Reporting cyber incidents, promoting cyber hygiene, supporting cybersecurity initiatives, and encouraging ethical hacking are ways in which individuals can actively participate in creating a safer digital environment.

Moreover, striking the right balance between convenience and security is an ongoing challenge. Being aware of potential trade-offs and making informed decisions while using digital services and technologies ensures that users do not compromise security for the sake of ease of use.

Embracing the cybersecurity mindset requires collaboration and cooperation among individuals, organizations, governments, and international entities. By working together, sharing threat intelligence, and collaborating on cybersecurity initiatives, we can build a resilient global defense against cyber threats.

In conclusion, the cybersecurity mindset is a call to action for individuals to be proactive, responsible, and engaged in safeguarding their digital lives. It involves educating oneself, adopting secure practices, advocating for cybersecurity awareness, and contributing to the well-being of the digital community. By embracing this mindset, we can collectively create a safer and more secure cyberspace for present and future generations. The path to a secure digital future begins with each individual's commitment to developing and nurturing the cybersecurity mindset.

B. The Continuous Journey of Strengthening Digital Defenses

In the ever-evolving landscape of cybersecurity, the journey of strengthening digital defenses is an ongoing and dynamic process. The threats we face today will undoubtedly change, becoming more sophisticated and unpredictable in the future. As technology advances, so too must our cybersecurity practices and mindsets. Recognizing that cybersecurity is not a one-time endeavor but a continuous journey is crucial for effectively protecting our digital assets and identities.

The conclusion of this book marks the beginning of a new phase—a phase of empowerment and commitment to cybersecurity. Armed with knowledge gained from understanding the cybersecurity mindset and its core principles, individuals are now better equipped to face the challenges of the digital world with confidence.

Strengthening digital defenses starts with acknowledging the potential vulnerabilities in our digital lives. It involves taking a proactive approach to identify and address weaknesses in our systems, networks, and online behaviors. Regularly conducting security assessments, risk analyses, and vulnerability scans is essential to stay one step ahead of potential threats.

Furthermore, organizations must adopt a cybersecurity-first culture that permeates throughout all levels of the organization. Employees should be educated and trained to recognize and respond to cyber threats effectively. Cybersecurity should not be seen as a burden but as an integral part of business operations and risk management.

Governments and international entities have a vital role to play in the continuous journey of strengthening digital defenses. Collaboration and information sharing among nations can enhance global cybersecurity resilience. The establishment of international cybersecurity norms and treaties can provide a framework for responsible behavior in cyberspace and deter malicious actors.

Continuous improvement in cybersecurity technologies is imperative. Innovations in artificial intelligence, machine learning, and advanced threat detection techniques can aid in identifying and mitigating cyber threats in real-time. Embracing emerging technologies while ensuring their security is paramount in this digital age.

As we navigate the complexities of the digital world, we must remain vigilant and adaptable. Cybersecurity threats are not static, and neither should our defenses be. Continuous learning and staying abreast of the latest developments in cybersecurity are essential for staying ahead of cyber adversaries.

Remember, cybersecurity is not a battle fought in isolation—it is a collective effort. By sharing information, best practices, and threat intelligence, we can foster a collaborative environment that strengthens the entire cybersecurity community.

In conclusion, the continuous journey of strengthening digital defenses is a responsibility shared by individuals, organizations, governments, and the global community. As we embark on this journey, let us embrace the cybersecurity mindset, be proactive in protecting our digital lives, and remain committed to building a safer and more secure digital world for generations to come. Together, we can create a resilient and trustworthy cyberspace that empowers innovation, creativity, and positive interactions while safeguarding against cyber threats. The journey begins now.

C. Empowering a Safer Digital Future

As we reach the end of this transformative journey through the world of cybersecurity, we are poised to shape a safer and more secure digital future. The knowledge gained from understanding the cybersecurity mindset and the core elements of cybersecurity provides us with the tools to protect ourselves, our communities, and the global digital ecosystem.

Empowering a safer digital future requires a collective effort that begins with each individual embracing the principles of cybersecurity. By adopting the cybersecurity mindset, we take responsibility for our online actions, recognizing the impact they can have on our personal security and the broader digital community.

At the core of empowering a safer digital future is the continuous commitment to education and awareness. By staying informed about the latest cyber threats, vulnerabilities, and best practices, we can make informed decisions and remain vigilant against emerging risks. Cybersecurity education should start early, empowering the next generation with the skills and knowledge they need to navigate the digital landscape safely.

Embracing emerging technologies holds immense potential for our digital future, but it also comes with risks. As we integrate technologies like artificial intelligence, the Internet of Things, and quantum computing, we must prioritize security in their design and implementation. Striking the right balance between innovation and security is essential to prevent potential disasters and ensure the trustworthiness of our digital ecosystem.

Collaboration and cooperation are pivotal in achieving a safer digital future. Public-private partnerships, international cooperation, and information sharing foster a collective defense against cyber threats. Cybersecurity is a global challenge that requires a united effort, transcending borders and ideologies to build a resilient and secure cyberspace for all.

Organizations must be at the forefront of empowering a safer digital future. By investing in robust cybersecurity measures, cultivating a cyber-aware workforce, and fostering a culture of security, organizations can protect their assets and customers while contributing to a safer digital environment overall.

Governments play a crucial role in shaping cybersecurity policies and regulations that safeguard citizens and businesses. By enacting legislation that promotes cybersecurity best practices and facilitates information sharing, governments can create a strong foundation for a secure digital future.

Ethical considerations must guide us in this endeavor. As we navigate the digital landscape, we must uphold principles of privacy, fairness, and accountability. Responsible disclosure of vulnerabilities, ethical use of technology, and respecting digital rights are essential to building trust and confidence in our digital interactions.

In conclusion, empowering a safer digital future requires the collective effort of individuals, organizations, governments, and the global community. As we move forward, let us continue to embrace the cybersecurity mindset, promote education and awareness, prioritize security in technology development, collaborate across borders, and uphold ethical principles in our digital endeavors.

Together, we have the power to shape a digital future that is resilient, trustworthy, and secure. By taking action now and building on the knowledge gained, we can create a digital world where innovation flourishes, individuals thrive, and our collective safety is ensured. The journey to a safer digital future has begun, and our commitment to cybersecurity will guide us toward a brighter tomorrow.